Encyclopedia of Transportation

Volume 2

Macmillan Reference USA/An Imprint of The Gale Group
New York

Macmillan Reference USA
1633 Broadway
New York, NY 10019

PRINTED IN THE UNITED STATES OF AMERICA
1 2 3 4 5 6 7 8 9 10

Library of Congress Cataloging-in-Publication Data

Encyclopedia of transportation.
  p. cm.
  "Editorial board: Enoch J. Durbin . . . [et al.]"--v. 1, p. .
  Includes bibliographical references and index.
  Summary: An encyclopedia covering different methods of transportation and key events, people, and social, economic, and political issues in the history of transportation.
  ISBN 0-02-865361-0 (6 vol. set)
  1. Transportation Encyclopedias. [1. Transportation Encyclopedias.] I. Durbin, Enoch. II. Macmillan Reference USA.
HE141.E53   1999
  388´.03--dc21   99-33371
                                                      CIP

Ballast

Ships, submarines, and hot-air balloons all require ballast to move properly. Ballast is any material used to add stability to a vehicle. Unlike cargo, ballast is valuable not for its own sake but for its effect on the vehicle.

A fully loaded cargo ship has enough weight below water level to be steered correctly. Once the cargo is unloaded, however, the ship bobs too high in the water and becomes difficult to steer. For centuries sea captains loaded ballast—generally in the form of stones or iron bars—into their ships' holds to correct this problem. Most modern ships are built with tanks that can be flooded with as much seawater as needed for ballast. Once the ballast is no longer required, the crew pumps the tanks dry.

Submarines also use the convenient supply of seawater for adding weight. When the crew floods the ballast tanks with water, the submarine dives. When water is pumped out of the tanks, the vessel rises toward the surface.

Hot-air balloonists use bags filled with sand as ballast. The weight of the bags adds stability to the passenger basket, which hangs below the balloon. The passenger can make the balloon rise by throwing out some of the ballast. For balloons without passengers, such as those used in atmospheric research, operators on the ground use remote controls to release some of the steel grit—a form of fine powdered steel—used as ballast. *See also* Balloons; Ships and Boats; Submarines and Submersibles.

Balloons

espionage spying

More than 100 years before the first airplane, people were flying for pleasure, adventure, scientific research, and even **espionage.** Borne aloft by balloons, they glided over cities, rivers, and borders. An early balloonist decorated his craft with the Latin slogan *Sic Itur Ad Astra,* "This Way to the Stars." Although balloons fell somewhat short of reaching the stars, they did make the age-old dream of human flight come true.

Balloons are basically large, airtight envelopes filled with hot air or a gas that rises and floats because it is lighter than air. The science of lighter-than-air craft is called aerostatics.

History of Balloon Flight.
The surprising thing about the invention of balloons is that it did not happen sooner. Since the time of the ancient Egyptians, various civilizations have known how to make paper or cloth through which air cannot pass. If a bag of such material is held over a fire and allowed to fill with heated air, it will rise, because hot air is lighter than ordinary air. The first recorded experiments based on this principle took place in 1709, when a Brazilian priest and inventor named Bartolomeu Lourenço de Gusmão may have made a small hot-air balloon. His work was little known and quickly forgotten. That would not be the case with the efforts of France's Montgolfier brothers.

In 1783 papermakers Joseph-Michel and Etienne Montgolfier launched the first hot-air balloons. One of their earlier balloons carried three barnyard animals, but a few months later, the Montgolfiers sent two Frenchmen aloft. This **ascension** over Paris, the first free flight by humans, lasted about 25 minutes. That same year another French

ascension rising, flight

People use hot-air balloons for sightseeing, military observation, and scientific research. Made of strong, lightweight materials, they can carry communications and surveillance equipment aboard.

aeronaut one who flies or travels in the air

team went up in a balloon filled with hydrogen, a gas that is lighter than air.

The American statesman and inventor Benjamin Franklin, who was then living in France, watched an early Montgolfier balloon ascension. He communicated his enthusiasm for ballooning to George Washington and Thomas Jefferson, who realized that the balloon would open up new possibilities for transportation, warfare, and science.

Early Uses of Balloons.
Balloons drew crowds and filled onlookers with wonder and excitement. Early balloonists toured as entertainers, sometimes performing stunts such as being carried into the air while riding horses or alligators. Then almost as soon as people began flying in balloons, they began jumping out of them. The first recorded descent by parachute took place in 1797. During the 1800s parachute jumps became popular attractions at fairs and shows.

The balloon was useful for more than entertainment. In 1785 two **aeronauts** crossed the English Channel between France and England in a balloon, carrying the world's first airmail letters. But because balloons cannot be steered and must go where the wind takes them, scheduled mail service by balloon was not practical. Balloonists also took the world's first aerial photos as photography developed in the early 1800s.

Military leaders immediately saw the advantage of sending someone up into the air with a telescope. Napoléon Bonaparte of France, one of the first to put the idea into practice, sent observers aloft in balloons that were tethered, or tied, to the ground. They could study the field of battle and report on the enemy's movements. Both sides in the American Civil

War used observation balloons. One was tethered above Washington, D.C., to give warning in case of a sneak attack on the capital. Balloons also served as airborne observation posts in World War I (1914–1918). During World War II (1941–1945), the Japanese tried, with little success, to start fires in North America by sending balloons armed with fire-bombs drifting across the Pacific Ocean.

Science, too, gained a new dimension with balloon flight. As early as the 1830s American balloonist Charles F. Durant made daring flights to study air currents over the Atlantic Ocean. Scientific use of balloons increased in the late 1800s, and by 1912 an Austrian scientist had risen to a height of about 3 miles to prove the existence of cosmic rays. In 1937 the U.S. National Weather Service began using balloons in **meteorological** surveys and weather forecasting.

meteorological having to do with weather

synthetic artificial, not found in nature

How Balloons Function.

Stripped to their basics, today's balloons are not very different from those of the Montgolfiers. They are airtight containers filled with hot air or a lifting gas. The most commonly used gases are hydrogen and helium. Modern envelopes are made of strong, lightweight **synthetic** fibers or plastics. Most are round, although envelopes designed for use on tethers may be cigar-shaped to reduce wind resistance.

Early aeronauts burned wool and straw in flight to keep the air in their balloons from cooling. Modern balloons have burners attached below them. A balloonist can make the craft rise at a steady speed by controlling the rate at which the burner operates. To descend, the balloonist pulls a line connected to a valve in the envelope. This releases the lifting gas, again at a controlled rate. If necessary—to avoid an unexpected obstacle on the ground, for example—an aeronaut can make the balloon rise suddenly by dropping ballast, or weight.

The Montgolfier brothers' barnyard animals ascended in a wicker basket slung below the balloon. The gondola, or car, of a modern balloon is also suspended below the envelope and burner. It can be a simple open basket or a closed capsule equipped with electronic communications devices and computerized navigational tools. But even the costliest and best-equipped balloons of today, like those of the 1780s, cannot be steered. Steerable lighter-than-air craft are called airships. Ironically, although airships overshadowed balloons in the early 1900s, few airships travel the skies of the world today, while balloons still have many uses.

First Flight in America

The first person to fly in the United States was a 13-year-old boy named Edward Warren. In 1784 he watched as a visiting Englishman named Peter Carnes sent an unoccupied balloon, tied to the Earth by a line, into the air north of Bladensburg, Maryland. The boy volunteered to go up in the balloon's basket. Warren's ride may have been a landmark in American flight, but Warren himself disappeared from the pages of history, and nothing is known of his later life. However, Carnes narrowly escaped death when his balloon struck a wall on a later flight in Philadelphia. He gave up flying.

Modern Uses of Balloons.

Balloons can be used in three ways—free, tethered, or controlled. Free balloons are released into the atmosphere with no passengers. Tethered or moored balloons are fastened to the ground by lines and may or may not carry passengers. Controlled balloons are free-floating and carry balloonists who control their lift and descent. Each type of operation is well suited to certain uses.

Recreational ballooning, for example, usually involves the controlled operation of a hot-air balloon. The later part of the 1900s saw tremendous growth in recreational ballooning. Travelers now can float high over scenic areas such as California's wine country or the wildlife-dotted

African plains, and balloon festivals and races attract both aeronauts and spectators.

Military forces still use tethered balloons as observation platforms and relay stations for communications signals. Because the cable that anchors a tethered balloon could endanger aircraft, such balloons are used only at low altitudes and in limited ways. Sometimes tethered balloons are put to commercial use, as when logging companies employ them to lift felled trees from places not reachable by road.

Zero-pressure balloons are free balloons that carry scientific instruments into the atmosphere. Governments and research groups launch several hundred of them each year for flights of between 8 and 40 hours. These teardrop-shaped balloons, made of a strong synthetic material called polyethylene, can lift heavy loads to heights of 140,000 feet above the Earth's surface, the doorstep of outer space. In fact, space scientists often use the gondola of a zero-pressure balloon for testing procedures, instruments, and technology intended for use on satellites or in the space shuttle.

Superpressure balloons are large free balloons that, once sealed, hold the same amount of lifting gas at all times. Although such balloons require extremely careful manufacture—a pinprick-sized hole can lead to loss of pressure—they have the advantage of being able to stay in the air for long periods. Some have remained airborne for more than a year. Instruments aboard superpressure balloons record air pressure, wind direction, and temperature. Transmitters on the balloons broadcast the data to orbiting satellites, which relay it to ground stations on Earth. Like the zero-pressure balloons, superpressure balloons provide a wealth of information to scientists studying atmosphere, weather, and climate. *See also* AIRSHIPS; BALLAST.

Up and Away

On March 20, 1999, Dr. Bertrand Piccard of Switzerland and Brian Jones of Great Britain accomplished a feat that balloonists had tried to achieve for 200 years. After 19 days, 21 hours, and 55 minutes aloft in the Breitling Orbiter 3 balloon, the pair became the first to complete a non-stop voyage around the world. Piccard and Jones started their journey in the Swiss Alps. They flew over North Africa, South Asia, the Pacific Ocean, Central America, and the Atlantic Ocean. By the time they landed in the Sahara desert of southern Egypt, they had covered approximately 29,055 miles (46,750 km). The historical flight succeeded in part because of advances in balloon technology and weather forecasting.

Baltimore and Ohio Railroad

Founded in 1827, the Baltimore and Ohio Railroad carried freight and passengers to and from the port of Baltimore—then the second largest city in the country. The B & O (as it was called) introduced a number of advances in rail technology, including steam locomotives.

The railroad was started with some urgency. After the opening of the Erie Canal in 1825, Baltimore merchants worried that the city's fortunes would suffer. The new canal enabled traders to send goods and raw materials between New York City and the newly settled American Midwest. Baltimore officials knew that if their city could not win a share of this trade, it would never become a great port. Because no major rivers flowed into Baltimore, they decided to build a railroad to the nation's interior.

The city of Baltimore, the state of Maryland, and a group of Baltimore traders joined to form the B & O and to finance its construction. The first section of track, 13 miles long, opened in 1830. After an unsuccessful experiment with railway carriages driven by wind sails, the line used horses to pull the carriages.

As soon as the railroad opened, the company's directors began to plan additional sections of track and to consider the use of mechanical power to move trains over long distances. In 1830 inventor Peter Cooper proved that the Tom Thumb, the first American steam locomotive, could handle the curves and uphill sections of the B & O. Over the next few years the railroad replaced all its horses with steam-powered engines.

The B & O expanded farther west, crossing the Appalachian Mountains and reaching its goal, the Ohio River, in 1852. By laying many miles of track and buying smaller lines, it became a major rail company, eventually providing service to Chicago, St. Louis, Washington, D.C., and New York. As it grew, the Baltimore and Ohio Railroad continued to introduce improvements, such as the first electric locomotives and the first air-conditioned passenger cars in the United States. In the 1960s it merged with the Chesapeake and Ohio Railway and later became part of the CSX Corporation. *See also* ENGINES; ERIE CANAL; RAILROADS, HISTORY OF.

Barges

At one time, barges were pulled by men, towed by animals, or propelled by wind in sails. Modern barges have engines or are pushed by tugboats.

Barges are spacious, flat-bottomed boats used for transporting cargo. Most barges carry bulky and heavy freight such as coal, oil, grain, gravel, steel, and waste materials. Used primarily on inland waterways or along seacoasts, they are not designed for transport on open seas.

Bargelike vessels have existed for thousands of years. In ancient Egypt, for example, barges transported people and goods up and down the Nile River. Propelled by rowers, these boats were sometimes elaborately decorated and used for carrying royalty. Through much of England's history, ceremonial barges played an important role in celebrations.

In the early 1800s, the United States went through a canal-building frenzy. Barges carried goods along the new waterways that linked rivers, lakes, and coastal waters. Because the canals were often no more than 50 feet (15 m) wide and 6 feet (1.8 m) deep, these boats had to be relatively small.

Before the invention of steam engines, canal and river barges were propelled by wind in their sails or pulled by people or animals walking along a towpath on the bank. Small barges could be towed by a pair of horses or mules, but large ones required teams of many animals. Even with several mules, these boats moved slowly—no more than 2 miles (3.2 km) an hour.

Although barges are still pulled by human or animal power in some parts of the world, engines propel most modern barges. In Europe large barges equipped with engines haul cargo along inland waterways. European barges often have rooms for crew members, making them more like regular ships.

In the United States, few large barges have built-in engines. Barges without engines—dumb barges—are generally pushed or pulled by tugboats, although sometimes the flowing current of a river supplies the power to move them. Dumb barges can be lashed together to form a single unit—called a tow—that is propelled by the tugboat. A single tow, consisting of as many as 40 barges, can transport many thousands of tons of cargo.

Whereas some barges haul freight over long distances, others perform specific tasks in one location. Dumb barges called lighters ferry back and forth in harbors, loading and unloading cargo from ships. Railroads use large barges to carry freight train cars across bodies of water that do not have bridges or tunnels.

Modern barges are built of steel or wood. Their size depends on where they are to be used and what type of cargo they are going to transport. For example, canal and river barges are limited in size by the width of the waterway and the curves along its route. Shippers use larger barges along seacoasts and on major lakes, such as the Great Lakes in the United States. *See also* ANIMALS, PACK AND DRAFT; CANALS; FREIGHT; HARBORS AND PORTS; SHIPS AND BOATS, TYPES OF; TUGBOATS.

BART (Bay Area Rapid Transit)

The Bay Area Rapid Transit—better known as BART—is one of the most advanced urban transportation systems in the world. Located in the San Francisco Bay area of California, BART's high-speed rail network links the major communities of that region. The computers of this fully automated train system control the speed and spacing of cars on the track, station stops, fare collection, and train announcements.

Construction of BART began in 1964, but its planning and design had started in the late 1940s when the city's population was increasing dramatically. The aim of the BART system was to help meet the growing transportation needs of the San Francisco Bay area in an environmentally sensitive way. One major goal was to decrease dependence on the automobile and thus reduce air pollution and highway congestion. The proposal also set forth a master plan to coordinate future transportation services in the region.

The BART project involved state-of-the-art design and engineering to meet the safety standards required for structures in this earthquake-prone area. The first section of track opened in 1972. Meanwhile, construction continued on the main link under San Francisco Bay, which consisted of concrete tubes laid in a trench on the floor of the harbor. Rail service below the bay began in 1974.

More than 81 miles (130 km) of its route connect BART's 37 stations. The system includes subways and tunnels, both surface and elevated rail lines, and the 3.6-mile (5.8-km) Trans Bay tube, the longest underwater tunnel in the United States. *See also* COMMUTING; LIGHT RAIL SYSTEMS; PUBLIC TRANSPORTATION; SUBWAYS (METROS); TRANSPORTATION PLANNING.

Bends

see Atmospheric Pressure.

Benz, Carl
German engineer

internal combustion engine *engine powered by burning a mixture of fuel and air inside narrow chambers called cylinders*

Carl Benz built the first successful automobile with an **internal combustion engine.** Born in Pfaffenrot, Germany, on November 25, 1844, Benz received an early education at a technical high school. After graduating, he found work with a machinist, and in 1871 he opened an engineering firm with a partner.

Benz began to pursue the idea of developing a motor vehicle but in early experiments made little progress toward that goal. He did, however, succeed in refining an industrial engine, and in 1883 he started a firm, Benz and Company, to produce it. The engine sold well, and Benz dedicated himself to building an automobile.

In this effort his chief rival was another German, Gottlieb Daimler. The two men—who worked independently and never met—had quite different approaches. Daimler believed that the public would accept automobiles only if they resembled horse-drawn carriages. Therefore, he focused on modifying existing vehicles. Benz, in contrast, felt strongly that horse-drawn carriages were a thing of the past, and he set out to build an entirely new kind of vehicle.

In 1885 Benz presented his first car, the Motorwagen. It had a bench seat over the engine, which was located in front of the two rear wheels, and a steering column to control the single front wheel. The car became popular, as did a four-wheeled model he introduced in 1893. Benz left his company in 1906 after disagreements with the board of directors and moved to Ladensburg, Germany, where he died on April 4, 1929. Three years earlier, Benz and Company had merged with Daimler's company to form Daimler-Benz, maker of Mercedes-Benz automobiles. *See also* AUTOMOBILES, HISTORY OF; DAIMLER, GOTTLIEB; ENGINES.

Berlin Airlift

In 1948 and 1949 the United States and Great Britain flew millions of tons of food and other supplies to the city of Berlin, which was located in the eastern, Soviet-occupied part of Germany. This Berlin airlift was the largest aerial supply operation in history.

After defeating Germany in World War II, the United States, Great Britain, France, and the Soviet Union assumed control of the country. The Communist Soviets took charge of eastern Germany and the eastern part of Berlin; the other three nations occupied sections of western Germany and the western half of Berlin. Postwar agreements allowed passage between Berlin—which lay completely within Soviet-controlled eastern Germany—and western Germany by means of narrow ground and air corridors.

Early in 1948 Britain, France, and the United States decided to combine their zones of Germany into a single unit. The Soviets regarded the creation of a unified western Germany as a threat to their own interests in the region. In protest, they set up a blockade of all highways and rail lines into Berlin in June 1948. The Soviets hoped that this action would force the Western powers to withdraw from Berlin so that the city could be united under Communist rule.

The United States and Great Britain responded to the blockade by launching an airlift of supplies to western Berlin on June 25, 1948. During the next year, British and American planes made more than 270,000 flights, delivering nearly 2½ million tons of food, fuel, and other supplies to the residents of the city. At the height of the airlift, planes were landing in West Berlin every few minutes.

Tensions remained high throughout the crisis, but the opposing powers avoided taking any action that might lead to war. Eventually the Soviets realized that their policy was not succeeding, and on May 12, 1949, they lifted the blockade. The airlift continued for several more months.

Soon after the Berlin airlift ended, the eastern and western portions of Germany were formally established as separate nations. Berlin remained divided and East Berlin became the capital of East Germany. The city of Bonn, located in West Germany, became the capital of that nation. Meanwhile, the United States and its allies hailed the Berlin airlift as a symbol of their determination to resist Communist expansion in Europe and elsewhere. *See also* AIR FORCES.

Bermuda Triangle

phenomenon an observable fact or occurrence

Fanciful writers have coined the names *Bermuda Triangle* and *Devil's Triangle* for an area of the Atlantic Ocean where many ships and planes have been lost. The imaginary triangle is formed by lines drawn between the island of Bermuda, southern Florida, and Puerto Rico.

Although people have suggested that mysterious and even supernatural forces are at work in the area, there is no reason to believe that anything other than natural forces and human error are involved. For one thing, the Bermuda Triangle is a place where variations in the Earth's magnetic field cause compasses to give readings that could confuse navigators. The other region where this **phenomenon** occurs, off the coast of Japan, has also been the site of unexplained disappearances. Second, the region's unpredictable weather and the varied pattern of reefs and trenches on the ocean's floor make navigation there difficult. Finally, the swift-flowing Gulf Stream runs through the Bermuda Triangle and may scatter debris and prevent searchers from locating wrecks and survivors. *See also* ATLANTIC OCEAN; GULF STREAM.

Bicycles

The two-wheeled, pedal-powered vehicles called bicycles are inexpensive, easy to operate and maintain. They require no fuel and create no pollution. For these reasons, people all over the world use bicycles for recreation, exercise, and transportation. Some countries have more bicycles than automobiles.

History of Bicycles

Invented in the 1800s, bicycles became very popular as people recognized their remarkable qualities. Cyclists could travel farther and faster on the new vehicles than they could go on foot.

The Birth of the Bicycle. The earliest ancestor of the bicycle was the *draisienne,* a vehicle with two wheels but no pedals invented in about 1817 by Baron Karl von Drais of Germany. The rider moved it forward by pushing his or her feet against the ground. About 20 years later a Scottish blacksmith named Kirkpatrick Macmillan built an improved version, adding a pair of foot-operated levers to a *draisienne.* The rider's feet swung the levers forward and back to pull the rear wheel around.

The French inventors Pierre Michaux, his son Ernest, and their assistant Pierre Lallement took the next step in the early 1860s, replacing the rear-wheel levers with front-wheel pedals that turned in a circular motion.

The bicycles of the 1860s, known as velocipedes or boneshakers, introduced a new style that had two pedals attached to the front wheel.

Bicycle Critics

Not all Americans welcomed the cycling craze of the late 1800s. Some preachers called it immoral, claiming that bikes allowed too much freedom for young men and women—and that too many people cycled instead of attending church on Sundays. Publishers moaned that people were riding more and reading less. The loudest outcries came from those who depended on horses for their livelihood, including stable owners and carriage makers. Soon, however, these trades faced a new and greater threat: the automobile.

This design, known as a velocipede, caught on in Europe and the United States, though its hard iron wheels earned it the nickname *boneshaker*.

In about 1870 English sewing machine manufacturer James Starley developed the high-wheeler, equipped with a small rear wheel and an enormous front wheel—up to 5 feet (2 m) tall. Wire spokes in the wheels and a frame constructed of steel tubes helped make it light and strong. Though the high-wheelers could go faster than earlier bicycles, they were somewhat unstable and dangerous. To dismount, a cyclist had to jump from the seat above the front wheel.

The safety bicycle, introduced in England soon after the high-wheeler, was easier for riders to manage. It had two wheels of the same size, with pedals attached to gears and a chain that turned the rear wheel. In the early 1890s bicycle makers switched from solid rubber tires to air-filled tires. They also settled on a frame design called the diamond or triangular frame. It consisted of a central triangle connecting the seat, handlebar, and pedals, with two smaller triangles securing the rear wheel. Few major changes appeared until the 1960s.

The Bicycling Craze. With the introduction of the safety bicycle, many people began pedaling. Many who could not afford horses and carriages could buy or rent bicycles. In Europe and the United States, bicycle clubs offered classes and encouraged people to take to the roads. Cycling became a favorite social and recreational activity.

Couples courted on bicycles—sometimes on tandem models that carried two riders. Doctors praised cycling as the perfect exercise. Women, who found the bicycle a convenient form of personal transportation, gained greater freedom. Female cyclists wore daring new clothes such as split skirts and baggy trousers called bloomers. People afraid to balance on two slender wheels preferred the three- and four-wheeled versions: tricycles and quadricycles. Nonriders could still enjoy the races that became popular spectator events. Adventurous cyclists constantly set long-distance touring records. From 1884 to 1886 a man named Thomas Stevens went around the world on a bicycle—except for the portions of the trip in which he had to push or carry his bicycle or travel by boat.

Few inventors could resist the idea of a motor-driven bicycle. Ernest Michaux experimented in the 1860s with a steam engine mounted beneath the rider's seat, but this dangerous vehicle did not succeed. The first American motorcycle was manufactured in 1901 using a gasoline engine, but soon automobiles surpassed motorcycles as the favorite form of transportation. Bicycle riding declined, though unlike the horse-drawn buggy, the bicycle remained a useful and efficient vehicle. In the 1930s bicycle riding became common among children, and beginning in the 1940s, cycling once again gained popularity with adults.

Types and Uses of Bicycles

Modern bicycles range in design and materials from lightweight touring models to sturdier versions intended for mountain and wilderness cycling. Riders include commuters, athletes, and children.

Equipped with sturdy frames and wide, knobby tires, mountain bikes can handle rough, unpaved surfaces.

Bicycle Parts and Operation. Early bicycles of the 1860s had heavy and clumsy frames and wheels, all made of wood and iron. Over the years new features and new materials made bicycles lighter,

Parts of a Bicycle

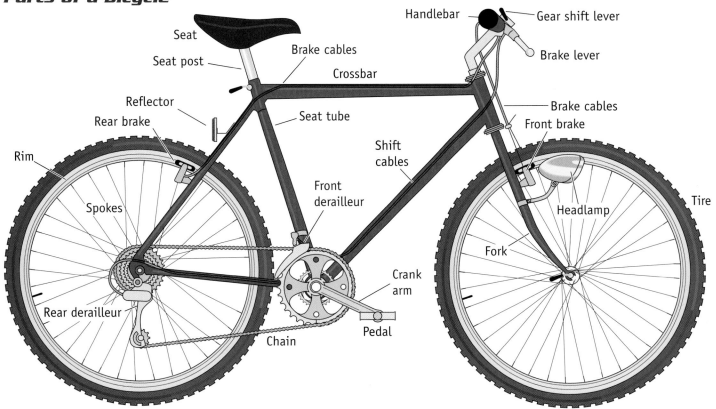

alloy substance composed of two or more metals or of a metal and a nonmetal

Tour de France

Every year spectators line the course of the Tour de France to watch cyclists compete in one of the world's most challenging races. Divided into more than 20 stages, the race lasts about three weeks. The roughly 2,500-mile (4,020-km) course tests riders' skill, strength, and endurance as they compete to win each stage and finish with the lowest total time. Excitement builds on the last day when the racers speed toward the finish line on the elegant Avenue des Champs Elysées in Paris. Cyclists from Europe usually win the Tour de France, although American Greg LeMond triumphed in 1986, 1989, and 1990, and American Lance Armstrong came in first in 1999.

faster, and more comfortable. Modern bicycles are built out of light-weight aluminum or metal **alloys,** carbon fiber, or other materials. Wheels consist of a rubber outer tire and an inflatable inner tube around a metal hub that is held in shape by thin wires called spokes. The cyclist uses a hand pump to maintain proper air pressure in the tube and a repair kit to patch holes in it.

The rider sits atop a column called the seat post, grips the handlebar, and steers the bicycle by using the handlebar to turn the front wheel. At the bottom of the seat post is the crank, to which the foot pedals are attached. As the rider pedals, the crank turns a gear that pulls a chain attached to the rear wheel and provides the bicycle's forward motion.

Most bicycles today have either coaster brakes or pressure brakes. Coaster brakes, often found on children's bicycles, require the rider to pedal backward to slow or stop the vehicle. With pressure brakes, the cyclist presses levers on the handlebars, activating the brake mechanism and causing hard rubber pads to press against the rims of the wheels. The resulting friction slows or stops the bicycle.

Shifting gears first appeared on bicycles in the early 1900s. The most common gears are sets of various sizes that carry the chain. Using a lever attached to the frame or handlebar, the rider causes an arm called a derailleur to shift the chain from one gear to another. Gears allow the rider to adjust the number of rotations made by the back wheel for each stroke of the pedal. Shifting the chain to a larger gear, for example, makes pedaling easier, but the rear wheel turns less often and progress is slower. Using a smaller gear, the cyclist can turn the rear wheel many times, producing greater distance and speed.

Bicycles may be equipped with a variety of additional features that contribute to the rider's safety and convenience. These parts include reflectors, lights, horns, air pumps, speedometers, cushioned seats, bottle holders, carrying racks, and baskets.

Types of Bicycles. Since the English inventor Alexander Moulton introduced a bicycle with small wheels, rubber shock absorbers, and a low frame in 1962, designers have constantly modified the structure of bicycles. Different types are well suited to certain uses.

Road bicycles are intended for riding on pavement. They have thin wheels and low handlebars that make riders lean far forward, reducing wind resistance. Certain kinds of road bicycles are specially designed for racing or for long-distance touring with luggage.

The mountain bicycle has enjoyed great popularity since the 1980s. It has a thicker, sturdier frame than the road bicycle, allowing it to withstand the shocks and bumps of rocky trails, and flat handlebars so that the rider sits upright. Its numerous gears and wide, knobby tires help the rider handle varied terrain, including mud and other unpaved surfaces.

Hybrid bicycles, which combine features of road and mountain bikes, are widely used for everyday activities such as commuting and shopping. They have flat handlebars and medium-width tires.

Other variations include tandem bikes for two pedaling riders; pedal-driven vehicles that can carry cargo or passengers; and recumbent bicycles, designed so that the rider leans back with the pedals out in front.

Recumbent bicycles make good use of the legs' energy. Recent developments include "comfort" bikes with fat tires and shock-absorbing seats and bikes that can shift gears automatically.

Cycling. After the introduction of the automobile, most Americans considered bicycles to be little more than pleasant diversions or children's toys. Since the 1960s, however, interest in cycling for sport, exercise, and transportation has increased considerably. In some years, Americans have bought more bicycles than automobiles. City planners now try to make provision for bicycle lanes in roadways and parks.

In some parts of the world, bicycling is the most common form of transportation. China and India produce millions of bicycles each year for their populations. In Denmark, the Netherlands, and some other European countries, a large percentage of workers commute on bicycles.

Safety is a vital element in bicycle transportation. In the United States cyclists must follow the same traffic rules as motorists. But bicycle riders are exposed to greater danger than automobile drivers and need to take extra steps to protect themselves. They should wear properly fitted helmets at all times, wear bright clothing or fluorescent vests that motorists can see, and use front and rear lights whenever visibility is poor. Above all, cyclists must ride defensively to avoid automobiles and other obstacles in the road. *See also* Mopeds; Motorcycles; Roads.

Blimps

see *Airships.*

Boats

see *Ships and Boats; Sailboats and Sailing Ships.*

Boeing

see *Aircraft Industry.*

Bridges

Bridges are structures that provide a pathway for humans or vehicles over obstacles such as rivers, lakes, or canyons. Bridges make transportation more efficient and convenient by sending traffic along more direct routes. Some of these structures have gained world renown as marvels of engineering or as models of grace and beauty.

History of Bridges

People have created bridges for thousands of years, beginning in all likelihood with logs placed across narrow streams and ravines. In some places they used natural bridges, such as formations of soil and rock that crossed an obstacle. Over time builders found ways to make wider and sturdier structures, for example, by setting wooden planks over crossing logs to form a walkway. Later they erected larger and more permanent structures with stones, bricks, and other materials. Archaeologists have found a wooden bridge in England dating from about 4000 B.C. The oldest known stone bridge, a stone slab that spans a river in Turkey, was built around 850 B.C.

The Romans. The greatest bridge builders of the ancient world were the Romans. They erected thousands of wooden, stone, and brick bridges as part of the road network that connected the provinces of their widespread empire.

The Romans excelled in the use of the arch—a curved structure of wedge-shaped stones fitted together—which could support great weight. By using several arches side by side topped with a flat roadway, they could construct long bridges.

The Romans also developed the cofferdam, a temporary enclosure made of upright logs driven into the bottom of a stream. When the inside of the cofferdam was pumped dry, workers could stand on the river bottom and build foundations for the bridge's vertical supports, known as piers.

People traveling in Europe still use a number of Roman bridges. One of the most famous is the Alcántara Bridge over the Tagus River in Spain, built in A.D. 98. Its six large arches span a distance of 600 feet (183 m), and it rises 175 feet (53 m) above the river.

Medieval to Modern Times. Bridge construction advanced very slowly during the Middle Ages. Builders continued to use the arch, and they learned how to strengthen bridge supports and foundations. Much of their effort, however, went to maintaining the old Roman structures.

Bridge building remained relatively unchanged until the introduction of iron construction in the 1700s. The first entirely cast-iron arch bridge was built in 1779 over the Severn River in England. Another new development of the 1700s was the caisson, an enclosure similar to the cofferdam except that it sank into the river bottom and became a permanent part of the foundation.

Since the 1800s bridge building has undergone remarkable advances. The use of new materials, such as steel and reinforced concrete, has

Roman Bridges

The ancient Roman bridges that are still standing provide glimpses of Roman engineering skill. The Martorelli Bridge in Spain, for example, spans 121 feet (37 m) and contains the longest remaining Roman arch. The Pons Mulvius in Rome, built around 109 B.C., was used repeatedly during World War II by troops crossing the Tiber River. Although it has been restored, it still includes four of the original arches. The Pont du Gard in Nîmes, France, was built by the Romans in 19 B.C. as part of an aqueduct to carry water. Consisting of upper and lower tiers, it measures 151 feet (46 m) at its highest point.

The Romans used arches of stone, wood, or brick to support the bridges they built.

Arch Bridge

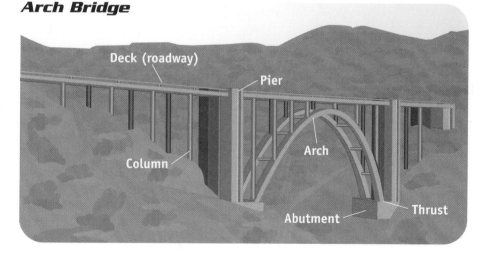

Deck (roadway)

Pier

Column

Arch

Abutment

Thrust

Suspension Bridge

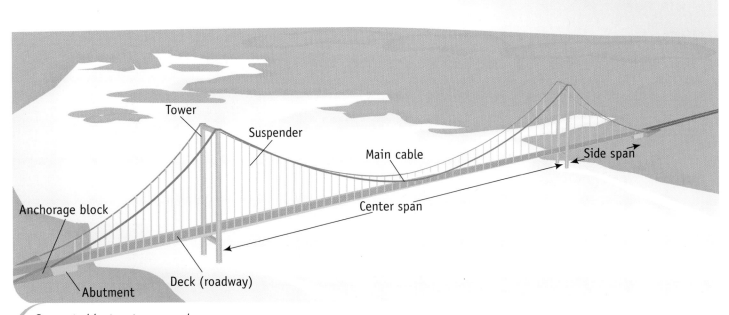

Tower

Suspender

Main cable

Side span

Anchorage block

Center span

Abutment

Deck (roadway)

Supported by two towers and a series of cables, suspension bridges can span great distances. Many of the longest bridges in the world, such as the Golden Gate in San Francisco and the Verrazano in New York City, use this design.

aerodynamics *branch of science that deals with the motion of air and the effects of such motion on planes and other objects*

abutment *support at the end of a bridge*

made the construction of longer, wider, and higher bridges possible. Architects and engineers designed various new types of bridges to carry trains and motor vehicles. Builders also incorporated principles of physics and **aerodynamics** to create stronger and safer bridges.

Types of Bridges

Bridges may be classified by their function—as railway bridges, highway bridges, or pedestrian bridges, for example—or by the materials used in construction. Another important classification is basic structure or design. The type of structure chosen for a particular site depends on such factors as the bridge's purpose, the materials available, the obstacle to be overcome, and the surrounding terrain.

Arch Bridges. The basic unit of all arch bridges, including those of the ancient Romans, is a curved structure built between two piers. The distance between two piers on any bridge is called a span. An arch bridge may have one span or many, depending on the number of piers and arches required to cross the obstacle. The use of steel has enabled engineers to design much longer arches than with stone or concrete. The bridge's deck, or roadway, may be constructed above the arch or suspended below with vertical beams or cables.

Girder Bridges. A girder is a large metal or wooden beam used in many types of construction. A girder bridge consists of a series of these beams placed side by side across the tops of piers and **abutments.** The girders support a road or railway. Girder bridges are generally used for short spans, including many highway overpasses in the United States.

Truss Bridges. A truss is a framework of triangles of metal or wooden beams that can support a great deal of weight. Truss bridge frameworks sit on top of piers; most bridges include two parallel trusses, one on either side connected by bracing. A series of trusses with additional piers can extend the length of the bridge. There are various kinds of truss bridges. Deck truss bridges, the most common type, are built with the roadway resting on top of the trusses. Through truss bridges have trusses that extend along the sides of the roadway.

Cantilever Bridges. A cantilever is a beam weighted or anchored at one end, which allows the other end of the beam to extend beyond its supporting pillar. In this type of bridge two cantilevers meet in the center of the bridge, usually connected by a structure called a suspended span. Each cantilever consists of two sections, or arms—one from the abutment to a pier in the middle and one from the pier to the far end of the cantilever. Modern cantilever bridges are made of steel and have trusses to give them added strength.

Suspension Bridges. With their distinctive curves and long spans, suspension bridges are often impressive sights. Instead of having a series of piers, they have only two tall towers, one on each side of the bridge. Thick cables hang between the towers and from each tower to an anchorage. Smaller cables, called suspenders, hang down from the two main cables to support the steel trusses of the roadway. A suspension bridge can span great distances. In high winds it is likely to sway slightly from side to side. The use of trusses helps stiffen the bridge.

Cable-Stayed Bridges. This type of structure resembles a suspension bridge because it has one or more tall towers and a deck suspended from cables. However, the cables of a cable-stayed bridge are connected directly from the towers to the roadway in fan-shaped patterns or other designs. This is a relatively new type of bridge, simpler and cheaper to construct than suspension bridges.

Other Types of Bridges. Some bridges have decks that move to allow ships to pass—by tilting, lifting, or swinging out of the way. A bascule bridge uses a system of weights to pivot upward from one or both ends. A vertical lift bridge has two towers with a roadway in between that stays horizontal as it rises. The deck of a swing bridge rotates from a central point.

The pontoon bridge is supported by floats, or pontoons. A roadway can be placed across a series of pontoons that are joined together and anchored to the bottom of a lake or river. Because pontoon bridges can be assembled quickly, armies often use them to provide temporary crossings for troops. Permanent pontoon bridges prove useful in places where it is difficult to build supporting piers for other types of bridges.

Major Bridges of the World

People have built bridges of all types and sizes throughout the world. The most famous are notable for their beauty, historical significance, engineering achievements, or record-breaking heights and lengths.

American Covered Bridges

The first covered bridge in the United States was built in 1806 over the Schuylkill River in Philadelphia. By the late 1800s, some 12,000 covered bridges dotted the American landscape between the Atlantic coast and the Mississippi River. The roofs and side walls on these bridges protected the wooden truss framework and flooring from harsh weather and provided welcome shelter for travelers. But as vehicles grew larger and heavier, iron and steel replaced wood construction. Even so, hundreds of covered bridges still survive as picturesque reminders of a younger America.

The United States boasts several major suspension bridges, including the Golden Gate Bridge across San Francisco Bay and the Verrazano-Narrows Bridge in New York City. The longest suspension bridge in the world is the Akashi Kaikyo Bridge in Japan, which spans 6,570 feet (2,000 m) between its towers.

Notable structures in other parts of the world include the historic Ponte Vecchio, an arch bridge in Florence, Italy, dating from 1345; the Firth of Forth Rail Bridge, a cantilever construction in Scotland; the Sydney Harbor Bridge, a steel arch bridge in Australia; and the Tatara Bridge, a cable-stayed bridge in Japan. *See also* AQUEDUCTS; FERRIES; RAILROAD INDUSTRY; ROADS; VIADUCTS.

Bullet Train

see High-Speed Trains.

Buses

A bus is a road vehicle designed to transport more people—generally between 10 and 70—than an automobile or van. In the United States, buses carry more passengers than any other form of public transportation. Traveling on existing roadways, they can provide comprehensive and flexible service in communities of all sizes. Most of them operate on a regular schedule over fixed routes.

The History of Buses

The history of buses began in Paris in 1662 with the introduction of horse-drawn carriages for transporting passengers. This service, however, lasted only a few months. Horse-drawn buses did not reappear until 1823, when the term *bus*—from the Latin word *omnibus,* meaning "for all"—was first applied.

Early Motor Buses. In 1830 an English inventor used a steam engine to produce the earliest self-propelled bus. The first gasoline-powered bus took to the road in Germany in 1895. The vehicle had an average speed of 9 miles per hour (14 km per hour), though its passengers occasionally had to push it uphill. By the early 1900s, motor buses had greatly improved, reaching speeds of 20 miles per hour (32 km per hour). Their popularity soared. Between 1904 and 1914, the number of buses in London increased from 20 to over 3,500.

The early vehicles had a bus body mounted on a truck **chassis.** Then in 1921 the Fageol Safety Coach Company of Oakland, California, produced a bus with a chassis specifically designed for bus service. It had a lower, wider, more stable frame. The low height also eliminated the need for a flight of steps to allow passengers to board the bus. Five years later the same company produced a bus in which the roof, floor, and sides were part of the structural frame, making the vehicle much stronger and safer. This design also featured twin engines placed beneath the floor of the bus between the front and rear axles.

chassis main body or frame of a vehicle

Technological Improvements. In 1927 the Mack Company introduced a bus frame with a floor lower than the tops of the wheels. This additional floor created luggage space below the passenger compartment, leading to wider use of buses for travel. The same year, Twin Coach built a bus with the engine at the rear, a design adopted by most of the industry. As buses grew in size, so did their engines—by the 1940s, 40-foot (12-m) buses with 12-cylinder engines were fairly common. The first bus powered by a diesel engine appeared in 1938. Diesel engines are still standard in modern buses.

Other changes increased the safety and convenience of buses and created the now-familiar look of buses produced until the 1960s. Manufacturers placed the front doors ahead of the front wheels and added another door closer to the rear, speeding the loading and unloading of passengers. Smaller wheels allowed for more interior space and gave buses a lower profile. Rounded corner windows and a windshield slanted inward at the top reduced reflections at night. Passengers could pull a cord attached to a bell to signal the driver to stop. Manufacturers also continued to unify the parts of the body and frame to reduce rattling and shaking and to make the bus lighter and stronger.

Bus ridership increased during World War II as Americans faced restrictions on gasoline use. But factories had to shift production priorities from **civilian** buses and cars to military vehicles. Military designs did lead, however, to significant improvements in buses after the war. In 1953 most buses received air suspension, pressurized air chambers mounted on each axle to dampen bumps and bounces. Unlike regular coil springs, air springs keep the level of the bus constant even as the weight of its load changes. Postwar buses also came equipped with better diesel engines, automatic transmissions, and air-conditioning.

A New Look. In 1959 General Motors introduced the "new look" bus that remained the standard for 20 years. These vehicles featured lightweight aluminum construction, larger windows and doors, fluorescent lighting, adjustable air brakes, and flexible seating patterns. During the 1970s, as part of an increased emphasis on public transportation, the U.S. government established new standards for bus construction. Many new companies emerged to produce buses for the anticipated growth in services.

Manufacturers continue to improve buses. Changes include wider doors and windows, lower floors, and new materials such as plastics and fiberglass. Many buses have wheelchair lifts or the capacity to tilt, providing easier access to elderly or disabled passengers. Another recent development is the use of articulated buses—made up of two cars connected by a flexible joint—that can carry up to 200 passengers. Although most still run on gasoline or diesel fuel, increasing numbers of buses are powered by alternative fuels such as natural gas, electricity, and hydrogen.

Bus Services

Bus service in the United States can be classified as city, suburban, intercity, and school. Different kinds of buses are generally used for different service.

civilian nonmilitary

"Leave the Driving to Us"

Started in 1914 with one driver in Hibbing, Minnesota, the Greyhound Corporation has grown into a fleet of about 2,100 buses stopping at more than 2,400 destinations. Greyhound also boasts a history of innovation. It was the first bus company to use diesel engines, rear-mounted engines, air suspension, central heat and air-conditioning, automatic transmissions, and onboard restrooms. Financial and labor problems hit Greyhound in the 1980s, but it remains the largest private bus company in the United States. Its famous slogan, "Leave the Driving to Us," expresses one of the major attractions of bus travel.

Buses carry passengers within cities as well as across regions. Federal legislation requires that buses manufactured after 1990 be accessible to people with disabilities.

Types of Buses.

City buses operate over short distances in urban areas, carrying people who do not own cars, dislike driving in heavy traffic, or have difficulty finding places to park. They typically have two entrances, low-backed seats, room for standing passengers, and no luggage space. Millions of people ride to and from work each day on city buses.

Smaller suburban buses make short trips between nearby cities or between a city and its surrounding residential areas. They tend to have a single entrance, luggage compartments or racks, and higher-backed seats than city buses.

Intercity buses operate between cities that may be several hours or even several days apart. These buses have higher and more comfortable seats, luggage space beneath the floor as well as in overhead racks, and a restroom on board. They may also contain amenities such as individual reading lights.

School buses carry up to 50 children each between their homes and schools. Resembling early motor buses, they usually have a bus body mounted on a truck chassis. They are equipped with special signal lights to alert other motorists when students are boarding or leaving the bus.

The Growth of Bus Service.

Before World War I, most people in the United States relied on commuter trains and trolleys for public transportation. Bus service grew rapidly during the 1920s with the development of larger, faster, and safer buses. However, in the 1930s bus ridership declined by one-third. The Great Depression put millions of people out of work and left many others too poor to travel. At the same time, the rise of automobiles allowed people to go where they wanted, whenever they wanted, without depending on bus routes or schedules.

During World War II, car travel was limited by gasoline and rubber rationing. As a result, bus use increased dramatically, reaching a peak of 25 billion rides a year. However, the end of the war marked the end of this boom. Rationing ceased, allowing large numbers of Americans to take to the road once again in their own automobiles. Another factor that cut into bus ridership—especially on intercity routes—was the growth of airline services between major cities.

During the 1960s and 1970s, in an effort to reduce pollution and traffic in crowded urban areas, the federal government spent hundreds of millions of dollars on public transportation systems. This financial support enabled some bus lines and manufacturers to stay in business. The Arab oil **embargo** of 1973 and the resulting "energy crisis" also played a role in the greater use of public transportation—and an increase in bus riders.

The Americans with Disabilities Act of 1990 requires that new public transit buses be accessible to people with disabilities, opening the way for a new group of riders. The continued expansion of suburban areas has led to a growth of regional bus lines. In the 1990s the number of intercity buses on U.S. highways increased to more than 675,000. Total bus ridership in urban areas, where many people commute to work each day by bus, reached nearly 4.7 billion rides per year. *See also* COMMUTING; GOVERNMENT AND TRANSPORTATION; PUBLIC TRANSPORTATION; URBAN TRANSPORTATION.

embargo government order prohibiting trade with another country

Cable Cars and Funiculars

Cable cars are vehicles that are pulled along the ground or through the air by a moving wire rope. Funiculars, a type of surface cable car, travel on very steep slopes. Whether on the ground or in the air, these vehicles are used to transport people and objects over steep or rugged terrain.

Horse-Drawn Cars. The cable car developed as an alternative to the streetcar, which first appeared in New York in 1832. Early streetcars were hauled along rails by horses and mules because, at the time, no engine had the power to pull a car loaded with passengers or cargo. Although these streetcars worked well in most cities, they were poorly suited for places with steep hills, such as San Francisco.

The First Cable Car. Andrew Smith Hallidie, an engineer from England, observed the difficulty of hauling the streetcars up San Francisco's hills. He noted that "four or five horses were needed for the purpose—the driving being accompanied by the free use of the whip . . . and occasionally by the horses falling and being dragged down the hill on their sides."

Hallidie had worked in California's gold mines. There he developed an extremely strong wire rope and invented a system, known as the Hallidie Ropeway, that used the rope to carry bins filled with rock and ore up and down the mines and across canyons. He realized that his ropeway could be used to pull streetcars up the hills of San Francisco.

Hallidie's plan called for a slot to be dug into the street all the way up a hill. In the slot, below street level, lay a wire cable that formed a continuous loop. The cable was driven at a constant speed by a large steam engine at the bottom of the hill. Each car was attached to the cable by means of a mechanical grip. When the grip was fastened, it held the cable tight and the cable dragged the car along, with rail tracks guiding the wheels. When the operator released the grip, the car was disconnected from the moving cable and stopped. The operator then applied brakes to

What Goes Up . . .

The principles used to drag cable cars to the top of the hill have been applied in building roller coasters. The world's highest roller coaster, the Fujiyama, towers 259 feet (79 m) over Yamanashi, Japan. Though not as high as the San Francisco hill where Andrew Hallidie constructed his first cable car line, the Fujiyama must travel a much steeper slope. Of course, when a cable car goes downhill, brakes carefully control its speed—but coaster riders are left to the mercy of gravity.

Cable Car

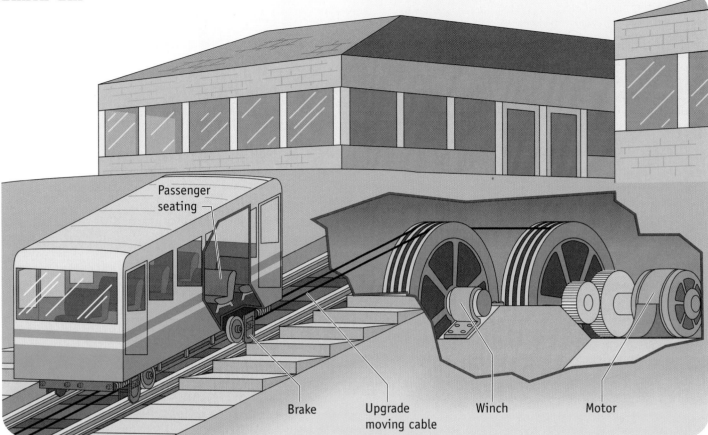

Passenger seating

Brake

Upgrade moving cable

Winch

Motor

Each car is attached to a moving cable by a mechanical grip. When the car reaches a stop, the operator releases the grip, applies the brake, and the car slows to a halt.

prevent the car from sliding downhill. This system enabled each car to stop independently of the others. At the end of the line, a rotating platform allowed the car to turn around and face in the proper direction.

Hallidie's plan faced widespread doubt and criticism, and the engineer had a difficult time raising enough money for the project. However, he finally managed to build a cable car line on San Francisco's Clay Street that was 2,800 feet (850 m) long and rose 307 feet (94 m) uphill. He tested it successfully on August 1, 1873. Cable cars quickly spread throughout San Francisco, as well as to other cities including Seattle, Chicago, St. Louis, Philadelphia, New York, London, and even Sydney, Australia. But by 1900 most cities began to abandon their cable car systems in favor of electric streetcars, sometimes called trolleys. Only cities with many steep hills continued to use cable cars. The cars, which still run in San Francisco, have become a popular attraction and a permanent part of the city's culture.

Modern Cable Cars and Funiculars. Today, cable cars are used more often on mountains than in cities. Funiculars work just like the urban cars, but they operate on much steeper runs. The car's **chassis** tilts back, parallel to the rail tracks, but the interior is built level with the horizon so that passengers and cargo can sit upright. Most funiculars have two cars operating at the same time; the weight of the car climbing the hill is balanced by the weight of the descending car.

chassis *main body or frame of a vehicle*

Cable cars are used mostly in mountainous regions. However, they continue to operate in the city of San Francisco and have become one of its main symbols.

Another common type of cable car is the aerial tramway, which is used to travel to and from great heights. The aerial tramway has cars fastened to a cable that is suspended in the air between two or more towers. The towers hold and guide the cable above the mountainside. In some cases, a single cable serves two functions: to support the car's weight and to move it forward. But for greater safety many tramways use two cables, one for each purpose. Tramways always keep the same number of cars ascending and descending in order to maintain equal weight on either side of the towers. Aerial cable cars are frequently used for sightseeing or to take hikers and skiers into mountainous terrain. The ski lift is one of the most common forms of an aerial tramway. *See also* LIGHT RAIL SYSTEMS.

Cadillac

Cadillac is the name used by the General Motors Corporation for its well-known luxury automobile. The name comes from Antoine de la Mothe Cadillac, the French explorer who founded the city of Detroit in 1701.

The Cadillac Automobile Company was created in 1902 when Henry M. Leland, a precision tool manufacturer, merged his firm with the Detroit Automobile Company. Known as the master of precision, Leland made Cadillac famous for comfort and superior engineering. He greatly improved the production of automobiles by introducing the principle of interchangeable parts. In 1908 he demonstrated the principle in London when he took three Cadillac cars apart, mixed the parts together, then reassembled and drove the three cars.

Although Leland's company was purchased by General Motors in 1909, it continued to be a leader in new technology. In 1912 Cadillac replaced the hand-cranked starter with an electric starter. Charles Kettering, its inventor, headed the company that produced these starters,

suspension system of springs and other parts that supports the body of a vehicle on the axles

running board narrow footboard on the side of an automobile

Delco Company. Two years later Cadillac offered the first V-8 engine, one of the standard engines used in cars. Other Cadillac firsts included safety glass, independent front **suspension,** air suspension, and fully automatic air-conditioning.

The company became a leader in automobile design as well. The 1938 Cadillac 60 Special was the first American car that could hold six passengers. To accomplish this, the designers made the body wider by eliminating the use of **running boards.** In the 1950s Cadillac became famous for lavish styling that featured large tail fins, pointed noses, and curved windshields inspired by aircraft design. Although Cadillacs built in recent years have a more streamlined shape, they still convey the image of luxury established by Henry Leland. *See also* AUTOMOBILE INDUSTRY; AUTOMOBILES, HISTORY OF; AUTOMOBILES, PARTS OF.

California Gold Rush

In 1848 a discovery in the foothills of the Sierra Nevada touched off an episode of mass migration that changed the history of California. The California Gold Rush brought people from all around the world to the American West by whatever means of transportation they could manage, giving an enormous boost to travel and commerce across the United States.

California was Mexican territory until 1848, when the United States defeated Mexico in a war and gained California and the Southwest. Many Americans had already settled in the region. In January 1848, just nine days before California officially became part of the United States, James Marshall, one of these settlers, found gold along the American River in the Sacramento Valley, about 40 miles (64 km) from the present-day city of Sacramento. He and his employer tried to keep the discovery a secret, but word reached San Francisco within a few months. By late summer people all around the world knew that there was gold in the California hills.

The first to flock to the area in search of fortune were the San Franciscans—the town's population dropped from 1,000 to about 100. Later, thousands of people, mostly men, arrived from the eastern United States and from Mexico, Europe, Australia, and China.

Some of those who came from the Atlantic Coast traveled overland along the Oregon Trail and a trail that branched off in Idaho and led south through Nevada and into California. Many could not afford a horse or wagon and walked the whole way, lugging their gear on their backs. Other hopeful prospectors traveled by sea. Some vessels made the long, hazardous voyage around Cape Horn at the southern tip of South America. Other ships landed on the east coast of Panama, leaving California-bound passengers to travel overland through the jungles of Central America and board another ship on the Pacific side. Because the first big wave of newcomers reached California in 1849, miners came to be called Forty-Niners.

Very few of the Forty-Niners won great wealth in the gold fields and mines. Each year thousands returned home, broke and discouraged. But those who found other employment and stayed boosted the population of San Francisco to 50,000 by 1856. Before the gold rush, the non-Indian population of California was about 14,000. By 1852, just three years into the gold rush, that number had swelled to more than 220,000, and California had become a state. *See also* OREGON TRAIL.

Camels

Camels are large mammals that people have used as saddle and pack animals since ancient times. Camel caravans were once the only way to transport goods across certain regions. In parts of North Africa, the Middle East, India, and central Asia, camels—sometimes poetically called ships of the desert—remain a vital means of transportation.

Although they originated in North America 40 million years ago, camels disappeared there about a million years ago. Two species of camel remained elsewhere in the world. The Arabian camel, also called the dromedary, was tamed by humans on the borders of the Arabian peninsula by 1800 B.C. The use of this long-legged, swift animal, which has one smallish hump in the middle of its back, spread to North Africa, the Middle East, and northwestern India.

The Bactrian camel, which is shorter and stockier than the dromedary and has two larger humps, is native to arid regions of central Asia, such as the Gobi Desert. Its thick, shaggy coat allows it to endure colder weather than the dromedary. Both types of camels have features that make them well suited to life in the desert—wide, soft feet for walking on sand, long eyelashes for protection against blowing sand, and the ability to close their nostrils, again for protection against wind and sand. The animals can graze on tough, thorny desert shrubs and grasses and can endure days, weeks, or even months without water because they obtain enough moisture from their food.

Dromedaries, good riding animals, can travel from 8 to 10 miles per hour (13 to 16 km per hour) for up to 18 hours. The Bactrian camels' double humps make them more awkward than dromedaries to ride, but Bactrians can carry loads of up to 1,000 pounds (450 kg). The typical load of the dromedary is closer to 600 pounds (272 kg).

In the mid-1800s people introduced dromedaries to Australia and both types of camels to the southwestern United States as beasts of burden. They were used in British Columbia in the 1860s during its gold rush. The wild descendants of imported dromedaries still roam the Australian outback. Camels fared poorly in America, however. Freight haulers who used horses and oxen resented the competition, and camels caused trouble by frightening other livestock. The experiment with pack camels in the American Southwest ended by the 1880s. *See also* ANIMALS, PACK AND DRAFT; CARAVANS.

Canadian Pacific Railway

transcontinental *extending across a continent*

The Canadian Pacific Railway was built in the late 1800s to link Canada's Atlantic and Pacific Coasts—a distance of nearly 3,000 miles (4,830 km). The idea arose while plans were being made for British Columbia to become part of Canada in 1871. When the people of this western territory asked for a road to connect them with the eastern provinces, the Canadian government promised to complete a rail line.

Because much of Canada was thinly populated, it was hard to justify the great effort and expense of building a **transcontinental** railroad. But officials in Canada hoped that the railroad itself would spur development and settlement. The first step—planning a route for the line—was not easy because little reliable information existed about Canada's central plains and western mountains. The planners hired engineer Sandford Fleming to conduct a massive survey across the continent and to recommend the best route.

In 1881 the government turned the project over to the Canadian Pacific Railway. Relying in part on Fleming's surveys, the company began linking together sections of track. The main line, from Montreal in the east to Vancouver in the west, was completed in 1885. After 1900, booms in agriculture, logging, mining, and immigration helped make the Canadian Pacific a success. The line became famous for its luxury passenger trains, which ran through regions of magnificent scenery. Vancouver, a logging town before the railroad arrived, became a major port city.

Over the years the railroad company—which changed its name to Canadian Pacific Ltd.—invested in other industries, such as timber, oil, gas, hotels, steamships, and airlines. In 1978 the company turned its passenger trains over to VIA Rail and limited its rail service to freight trains. By the late 1900s, the railroad was only a small part of Canadian Pacific's activities. *See also* Railroads, History of.

Canals

A canal is an artificial waterway, usually linked to one or more natural bodies of water. For thousands of years canals have been built to move water to areas where it is needed and to carry boat, barge, and ship traffic. Some of the largest and most impressive works of human engineering, both ancient and modern, have been canals.

History of Canal Building

The earliest canals were probably built to provide water for irrigating crops and for drinking. Only later did people begin sailing vessels on canals and then constructing them specifically for maritime traffic.

Early Construction. The practice of canal building was established early in the dry lands of the ancient Near East, where irrigation was necessary to support farming and livestock raising. Large-scale canal systems were usually the work of strong central governments, such as those of the Phoenician, Sumerian, and Babylonian empires. In the 600s B.C. the king of Assyria ordered the construction of a 50-mile

Further Information
To learn more about the construction and use of specific canals, see the related articles listed at the end of this entry.

(80-km) canal to bring water to the city of Nineveh. The Egyptians, meanwhile, had built a waterway across the desert between the Nile River and the Red Sea. This canal, which allowed travel between North Africa and the Indian Ocean, remained in use on and off for centuries.

The powerful and highly organized Roman Empire, which launched many large engineering and public works projects, built canals in North Africa, Italy, northern Europe, and Britain. Some of these were irrigation canals that transformed deserts into fertile farmland. Many others were constructed to improve transportation, especially the movement of military troops. After the fall of the Roman Empire, canal building in Europe suffered a decline that lasted several hundred years.

On the other side of the world, in China, canal construction was an important aspect of public engineering. As early as the 500s B.C. the Chinese were digging canals for irrigation and flood control along the Yellow and Yangtze Rivers. Over the centuries various canals became part of a transportation and commerce network called the Grand Canal that linked the northern and southern parts of the country. By the A.D. 1200s the Grand Canal measured some 1,000 miles (1,610 km) and was the longest artificial waterway in the world.

The Great Age of Canal Building. The rise of commerce in Europe led to a spurt of canal building in the 1100s and 1200s. Belgium and the Netherlands developed large networks of waterways that drained the low-lying flatlands and carried boats and barges. The

Canal building flourished in the 1820s and the 1830s to meet the demand for better forms of transportation between coastal regions and the interior.

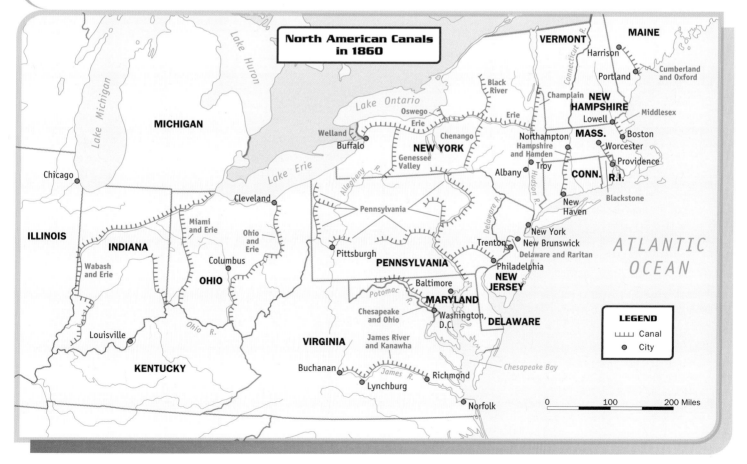

North American Canals in 1860

LEGEND
⊔⊔⊔⊔ Canal
● City

0   100   200 Miles

Languedoc Canal of France was completed in 1692. This engineering marvel connected the Atlantic Ocean and the Mediterranean Sea by linking two rivers with a series of aqueducts, reservoirs, tunnels, and locks.

During this time, Europeans made an effort to improve natural waterways by widening, straightening, or deepening them to handle shipping traffic and to remove hazards such as rapids. This process is known as canalizing a river. Although canalized rivers were central to the development of inland waterways, the dawn of the industrial era in the mid-1700s brought an increase in the construction of entirely new canals to extend the waterway systems.

In England the Duke of Bridgewater built a canal in 1761 to carry coal from his mines to the industrial center of Manchester. Other canals followed, and by the mid-1800s a network of waterways crisscrossed the British Isles like a spider's web, carrying raw materials to factories, food and fuel to cities, and manufactured goods to ports. During the 1800s Sweden, Russia, Germany, and Italy all enlarged their transportation systems with new inland canals, and the Netherlands opened several new canals for traffic between the North Sea and the interior of Europe.

In North America, canal building flourished after 1800 as settlement and trade moved westward. The 363-mile (584-km) Erie Canal, completed in 1825, linked the Hudson River to the Great Lakes, making it possible for Americans to ship heavy freight by water between New York City and the Middle West. The first section of Canada's Welland Canal, which connected Lakes Erie and Ontario, opened in 1829. By 1848 a network of canals laced the eastern part of the United States, connecting eastern rivers and seaports with the Great Lakes and the Ohio and Mississippi Rivers to form a vast transport system.

Major Modern Canals. Three of the biggest canal-building projects in modern history were undertaken to allow oceangoing ships to pass from one sea to another. French engineer Ferdinand de Lesseps designed the Suez Canal, a 103-mile (166-km) waterway between the Mediterranean Sea and the Gulf of Suez. Completed in 1869, it allows large ships to move from Asian to European waters without traveling around Africa. The Suez Canal inspired the building of Greece's Corinth Canal. This deep trench, finished in 1893, provides ships with a shortcut between the Ionian and Aegean Seas. Lesseps also began work on a waterway through Panama in Central America. But it was the United States that completed the Panama Canal in 1914. The canal allows freight, passenger, naval, and fishing craft to cross between the Atlantic and Pacific Oceans, bypassing the long and difficult voyage around South America.

Canal Construction and Operation

Before building begins, the planners must decide where the canal should run and what functions it will serve. A canal should follow the straightest and flattest possible course. One that ascends or descends will require locks to adjust the water level. If the canal is to be used for travel and shipping, it must be wide and deep enough for the vessels that will use it.

By Rail and Water

Pennsylvania's "Main Line," which opened in 1834, was an engineering wonder that used the two main transportation methods of the day. Built to link the East Coast with the interior basin west of the Allegheny Mountains, the Pennsylvania Canal and Railroad covered a distance of 394 miles (634 km) between Philadelphia and Pittsburgh. It consisted of two short pieces of railroad and two longer stretches of canal and river boating. The railways hauled sections of the canal boats, which were then lowered into the water and clamped together to float along the waterways. Passengers and freight could make the entire journey in a single vessel.

The Panama Canal, completed in 1914, connects the Atlantic and Pacific Oceans. In this photo a ship is being towed through the Miraflores Lock between Gatun Lake and the Bay of Panama.

Building a Canal.
Construction is primarily a matter of digging a deep trench through earth and rock. Unless the canal runs through solid rock, it may need a lining of clay, crushed rock, asphalt, or concrete to keep water from leaking into the surrounding soil. The canal may also require bridges.

Many canals and canalized rivers depend on dams and reservoirs to provide an adequate supply of water, especially for their upper stretches. In some cases these dams also serve as sources of hydroelectric power. From time to time canals need to be cleaned by dredging or other means to keep them free of **sediment** and **obstructions.**

sediment *material that settles to the bottom of a liquid*

obstruction *something that gets in the way*

Canal Locks.
A canal lock is basically a chamber—sometimes big enough to hold several large ships—with watertight gates at each end. It allows boats to navigate between stretches of water at different elevations.

A vessel moving from a lower to a higher water level enters the lock after the water has been brought down to the low level. As the lower gate closes behind the boat, the upper gate opens, allowing water to flow into the chamber. When the water reaches the level of the upper stretch of canal, the vessel can proceed on its way. To travel in the opposite direction, the boat enters the lock when the water is at the higher level. The upper gate closes, the lower gate opens, and water drains out of the lock until the boat is on the same level as the lower stretch of canal.

The Decline of Canals

The advance of railways in the mid-1800s spelled the end for many canals. Trains could move freight faster than canal boats and barges, and railways were easier to build than new canals. In addition, railway companies lowered their shipping rates to lure customers away from the canal carriers. By 1900 half the canals in the United States had closed. So had many British canals, bought up by the railways. During the 1900s, highway trucks offered yet another alternative for freight transport.

The effect of railways and highways was less severe in Europe, where canals continued to play an important role in the transportation system. Some countries built new canals. France, for example, doubled its canal traffic between 1900 and 1939. Waterways still play an important role in commerce, especially when the speed of transport is less important than the cost. Shipping by canal is slower but cheaper than shipping by truck or rail. The busiest artificial waterways today are the large international sea-to-sea canals, such as the Suez and Panama, and those that are part of river and lake networks such as the Mississippi River and Rhine River systems. *See also* BARGES; ERIE CANAL; LESSEPS, FERDINAND DE; PANAMA CANAL; SHIPPING INDUSTRY; SUEZ CANAL.

Canoes and Kayaks

Canoes and kayaks are small, narrow, lightweight boats usually powered by one or two people with paddles. They have been used since ancient times to transport passengers and goods, and they remain in use today, mostly for recreation.

Origins and Types of Canoes. The oldest form of the canoe was probably the dugout, a boat produced from a single log. A person can make a dugout by removing branches from a log, shaping its ends to points, and hollowing out the middle with fire or tools. The dugout works well in shallow waters, where a passenger can stand inside the vessel and push a long pole against the bottom of the river or lake.

The dugouts of New Zealand's Maori people were large enough to carry groups of warriors. Pacific Islanders added **outriggers** and made long voyages between island chains in the Pacific Ocean. Native Americans of the Pacific coast, the southeast Atlantic coast, and the Caribbean also relied on dugouts for travel and fishing. Similar boats are used in some parts of the world today.

Indians of northeastern North America developed the much lighter birch-bark canoe, which had a framework of branches and an outer hull of tree bark. **Portage** was easy with such boats, which could carry a considerable amount of cargo.

Farther north, the Inuit of Alaska and the Arctic coast developed the kayak, with waterproof seal hides stretched over a frame of wood or whalebone. The kayak's covering extended over the top, preventing water from splashing into the boat. The paddler sat flat in the kayak with outstretched legs, upper body emerging from a hole in the hides. The covering was so snug that paddlers could roll the boat completely over without losing their seats or taking on water—a movement that modern

outrigger *parallel float attached to the side of a boat to make the boat more stable*

portage *transport of boats and supplies overland between waterways*

kayakers call the "Eskimo roll." The Inuit used the kayak for hunting and a larger, open-topped canoe called the umiak for transporting families and cargo.

Modern Canoes and Kayaks.

Modern boatbuilders create canoes and kayaks from a wide variety of materials, including metal, fiberglass, and plastic. Nearly all canoes are pointed at their ends, but some are made with a flat end to which a small motor can be attached. A key issue in canoe and kayak design is the balance between maneuverability—ease of steering—and stability. A boat with high, round ends should be easy to **maneuver;** one with low ends and a flat bottom should be stable.

Paddles come in various shapes. A canoe paddle has a blade at one end and a handgrip at the other. The canoeist generally makes all strokes on the same side of the boat, often balancing a partner who rows on the other side. A kayak paddle has a blade at each end, and the kayaker alternates strokes on each side.

Uses of Canoes and Kayaks.

For centuries, dugouts, canoes, and kayaks were working boats that carried fishers, hunters, warriors, and cargoes in many parts of the world. When Europeans began exploring and colonizing North America in the 1500s, they quickly realized that the light birch-bark canoe was the perfect way to travel over the continent's many rivers and lakes. French colonists along the St. Lawrence River built canoes for the trappers and traders involved in the region's booming fur trade. The canoe made the fur trade possible. Much of North America was explored by canoe, and some surveyors and park rangers still rely on canoes and kayaks in their jobs.

However, most modern paddlers use these boats for recreation. They generally divide their sport into flatwater boating and whitewater boating. Flatwater boating takes place on lakes or quiet rivers; whitewater boating consists of paddling through rapids while avoiding rocks and other obstacles. Canoe and kayak touring often involves multiday trips along rivers. Modified vessels called surf kayaks and sea kayaks can be used on the ocean, where large waves can easily overturn a canoe.

The growth of recreational canoeing and kayaking has spawned many new products for paddlers. For instance, the kayaker may wear a sprayskirt—a garment that attaches to the upper surface of the boat and forms a watertight seal. However, any paddler's most important piece of equipment is the personal flotation device, or safety vest. *See also* SHIPS AND BOATS, HISTORY OF.

For centuries canoes have been used for transportation on rivers, lakes, and other shallow bodies of water.

maneuver to make a series of changes in course

Cape Canaveral

In 1947 the U.S. military relocated its long-range missile testing from White Sands, New Mexico, to Cape Canaveral, a small peninsula on the Atlantic coast of Florida. The new location offered several advantages, including the possibility of launching rockets eastward over the Atlantic Ocean, where accidental crashes would cause no damage. Moreover, a string of small islands extends several thousand miles eastward from the cape, providing ideal sites for tracking stations.

The space complex at Cape Canaveral includes launch facilities, assembly buildings, and storage and repair sites. The photo shows a group of specialists in the mission control room monitoring a shuttle.

facilities *something built or created to serve a particular function*

NASA *National Aeronautics and Space Administration, the U.S. space agency*

Early Years of the U.S. Space Program.
Cape Canaveral developed from a testing site for missiles to the center of the U.S. space program. Construction of **facilities** was not easy—the cape consisted mainly of mosquito-infested swamps and marshes, with Patrick Air Force Base at one end. After its creation in 1958, **NASA** leased space from the Air Force to pursue its program of both crewed and uncrewed spaceflights.

NASA's facilities on the cape were renamed the John F. Kennedy Space Center in 1963 in honor of the assassinated president. The following year NASA expanded onto Merritt Island, which could accommodate larger rockets. The island lies between the cape and the mainland, and the entire area is known as Cape Canaveral.

Launch Facilities.
By the time of the Gemini and Apollo missions in the late 1960s and early 1970s, the basic layout of launch facilities had been well established. The individual pads draw pressurized gas and liquid fuel from nearby storage tanks. Each pad has a large service tower that surrounds the rocket, giving technicians access to every part of the rocket. The tower also provides electrical and mechanical connections for fueling, instrument controls, and other needs. It is rolled back before liftoff. Most launchpads have a nearby "burn pond," into which liquid fuel can be dumped if a mission is postponed.

The Johnson Space Center in Houston, Texas, now serves as mission control for all crewed spaceflights after they are launched from Cape Canaveral. Following the launch, networks of tracking stations in the Atlantic Ocean and around the world monitor the spacecraft's progress by radio and radar.

Cape Canaveral Today.
Cape Canaveral is now a sprawling complex of assembly buildings, control centers, launchpads, hangars, and runways. The site is dominated by the 52-story Vehicle Assembly

orbiter *piloted section of a space shuttle that goes into space*

probe *uncrewed spacecraft sent out to explore and collect information in space*

Building, where Saturn rockets and Apollo spacecraft were assembled for lunar missions and where **orbiters,** external fuel tanks, and rocket boosters are prepared for space shuttle missions. Many rockets carrying satellites and space **probes** continue to be launched from Cape Canaveral. *See also* ROCKETS; SPACE EXPLORATION; SPACE SHUTTLES; SPACE TRAVEL.

Cape to Cairo Railroad

Transportation is sometimes closely linked to politics. An example is the Cape to Cairo railroad in Africa—a railroad that was never built.

The railway was the dream of Cecil Rhodes, a British financier and politician of the late 1800s. In 1890 Rhodes became prime minister of the Cape Colony, a province of South Africa that was controlled by Great Britain. He believed the British could promote their interests in Africa by building a railway from the continent's north coast—starting at Cairo in Egypt—to the Cape of Good Hope at its southern tip. The railroad would transport goods, settlers, and soldiers.

Not everyone shared Rhodes's dream. Italy, France, Belgium, Germany, and Portugal all had interests in Africa at the time, and all opposed the proposed British railway. Not until the mid-1900s did a rail line link South Africa with the Congo in the middle of the continent. There is no rail connection between Cairo and the Cape, although airplanes and motor vehicles now travel between them.

Car

see Automobiles.

Caravans

A caravan is a group of people and pack animals traveling together by land. Travelers often joined caravans for safety in numbers when crossing dangerous territory. Their destinations included religious shrines, trading centers, and new settlements. Caravans were common well into the 1800s.

In caravans across the deserts of North Africa, the Middle East, and central Asia, camels served as pack animals. Travelers slung their possessions or baskets for passengers on each side of the camel. When possible, caravans stopped at large compounds called caravansaries, where the animals stayed in an open courtyard while the people rested in surrounding rooms.

Some of the biggest caravans formed to bring Muslim worshipers to the holy city of Mecca in the Arabian Peninsula. Such caravans included up to 10,000 camels. Traders crossing the Sahara in North Africa used as many as 20,000 camels at a time, as they made their way from the Mediterranean coast to cities such as Timbuktu and Gao in what is now Mali. Caravans also traveled the Silk Road, a trading route from the Middle East to the markets of India and China. Such journeys often took months because the caravans tended to move at only about 2 to 3 miles per hour (3 to 5 km per hour).

In North America caravans crossed the Great Plains in the 1800s. Drawn by a desire to find gold, open land, or religious freedom, settlers joined together for the long trip west. Guides led travelers and their horses, oxen, and mules along the Santa Fe Trail, Oregon Trail, or other routes. Caravan travel declined as ships and railroads offered safer, quicker, and cheaper forms of transport. *See also* CAMELS; OREGON TRAIL; SANTA FE TRAIL; SILK ROAD.

Caravels

see Sailboats and Sailing Ships.

Careers in Transportation

People and goods move constantly in modern societies, and the efficient operation of the world's economies depends on fast and reliable transportation. Millions of people hold jobs related to transportation. Some jobs, such as that of airline pilot and truck driver, are fairly obvious, but many other less familiar or behind-the-scenes positions are just as important.

Further Information
To learn more about the types of work people do in particular transportation industries, see the related articles listed at the end of this entry.

Motor Vehicle Transportation

Motor vehicles include cars, buses, trucks, motorcycles, and other vehicles that travel on roads. Careers in motor vehicle transportation fall into four basic areas: manufacturing; sales, rentals, and service; traffic control; and driving.

Manufacturing. This area includes the design, testing, and construction of motor vehicles. Some people working in design focus on research—developing construction materials, adapting machinery, and devising manufacturing processes. Others are responsible for creating and testing new vehicle designs. Careers in these areas generally require college degrees in such fields as engineering, chemistry, physics, and industrial design. Some jobs may call for artistic ability and creativity as

Automotive engineers work together to create designs for new vehicles and systems.

well as mechanical and engineering skills. Experienced individuals with knowledge in areas such as finance or marketing can move into company management.

Other careers in manufacturing involve the assembly of motor vehicles or the parts from which they are made. To prepare for jobs requiring skilled labor—that of machinist, pattern maker, and tool and die maker—workers spend several years of apprenticeship under experienced employees. Their training may also include classes in mathematics, computer technology, and drafting. Unskilled jobs, such as **assembly line** positions, usually require a high school diploma and perhaps a background in mathematics or industrial arts.

assembly line production system in which tasks are performed in sequence by an arrangement of workers and equipment

Sales, Rentals, and Service. A persuasive personality and the ability to deal well with people will be helpful to anyone interested in a career in motor vehicle sales or rentals. Knowledge of the product to be sold is vital. Sales experience is beneficial, as is college training in business. Not all sales jobs involve selling vehicles; some people work with garages and car dealers that purchase automobiles. Practical and mechanical experience with cars and car parts is especially useful to such salespersons.

People who work in motor vehicle service—including auto mechanics—generally learn their skills from experienced workers, often at vocational schools. Mechanics employed by car dealers may be trained by special instructors from auto manufacturers. At car dealerships, service managers schedule repair jobs and assign them to individual mechanics. Managers usually have both mechanical experience and some business or management training.

Traffic Control. Safe and well-designed transportation networks are essential for traffic control. Traffic engineers plan and manage highway systems or bus and subway lines for government agencies or private corporations. Taxi, truck, and bus companies all employ dispatchers, who coordinate the movement of vehicles on the road.

Driving. The most visible jobs in motor vehicle transportation are those of the professional drivers who operate taxis, buses, trucks, delivery vans, and other vehicles. Such jobs do not require formal education, but many involve specialized training in operating vehicles properly and safely. Professional drivers must also obtain special commercial driver's licenses.

Railroad Transportation

Rail transportation workers operate and maintain trains, subways, and streetcars. Positions range from those of highly skilled engineers and vehicle operators to those of conductors and their assistants. Railroads also employ civil and electrical engineers, lawyers, marketing professionals, and computer experts. Overall planning of rail systems is handled by transportation engineers and planners who work with government agencies or railway companies to coordinate routes. The increasing use of computers in rail systems operations has caused a decline in the number of rail transportation workers.

Engineers. Railway engineers operate the controls that make trains start, accelerate, and stop. They monitor the gauges that measure speed, temperature, fuel, and other aspects of a locomotive's performance. They keep watch over warning signal systems and track and train conditions. They also check locomotives for possible mechanical problems. Subway and streetcar operators have some of the same responsibilities for their vehicles.

Many railway engineers start their careers as assistant conductors or conductors. They attend classroom training programs to learn more about locomotive equipment. Individuals who want to be engineers should be physically fit and have good eyesight, hearing, coordination, and mechanical ability. They must undergo periodic evaluation to determine their fitness for their jobs. Subway and streetcar operators usually receive special instruction focusing on the transit system and safety procedures.

Conductors. Conductors on freight trains keep records of the train's contents and destinations and make sure that cars are added or removed at the proper points along the route. On passenger trains conductors collect fares, assist passengers, and signal engineers when to leave the station.

Conductors receive information via radio about track conditions or operating instructions and pass them along to engineers. Some of the information comes from other railroad employees who inspect trains to make sure they are in good running condition. Assistant conductors add or remove cars from a train and switch trains from one track to another under the supervision of a yard conductor.

Conductors usually learn their skills on the job. On some railroads, they receive extensive training in their various duties. Conductors usually start as assistants and must pass tests about signals, timetables, and other aspects of railroad operation.

Air Transportation

Civil aviation offers a wide variety of career opportunities, from highly technical jobs such as airline pilot, aircraft designer, or air traffic controller, to jobs that require little special training such as baggage handlers and flight attendants. Airlines and airports offer employment in areas related to civil aviation. Many jobs in the field are based at airports. Airport managers oversee airport operations and work with airline executives and local officials to plan for future growth. The armed forces provide opportunities in military aviation.

Pilots. Some pilots fly large commercial passenger or cargo planes. Others operate small aircraft, carrying passengers and cargo or engaging in activities such as aerial rescue, crop dusting, traffic monitoring, and flight instruction.

Keeping an Airship Aloft

One of the more unusual forms of transportation is the airship—a lighter-than-air craft also known as a blimp. Although airships carry only about six passengers in their compact cabins, launching, flying, and safely landing one involves a crew of as many as 15 riggers, mechanics, ground handlers, and electronic technicians. The slow-moving ship is easily blown about by air currents and responds hesitantly to the pilot's efforts to change direction. But a blimp's gentle cruising speed and low flying altitude provide an enjoyable ride for everyone on board.

Large commercial airplanes often have two pilots—a head pilot, or captain, and a copilot. Captains have chief responsibility for operating the aircraft and supervising the crew. Copilots assist captains in flying the plane. They monitor cockpit instruments and communicate with ground personnel. Some large aircraft also have flight engineers—less experienced pilots who operate various instruments and assist the plane's pilot and copilot. Before taking off, pilots check to make sure that the plane's controls, instruments, and systems are working properly.

Pilots of small aircraft have similar responsibilities. They may also have nonflying duties, such as helping to load and unload passengers and cargo, supervising refueling, keeping flight records, arranging for maintenance, and doing minor repair work.

All pilots who carry passengers or cargo need a commercial pilot's license issued by the Federal Aviation Administration (FAA). To qualify, applicants must have a minimum of 250 hours of flying experience and take written and flight tests given by the FAA. They must also pass a rigorous physical examination and be in good health. Many commercial pilots gain their flight training and experience while serving in the military. Individuals can also receive flight training in programs at flying schools certified by the FAA.

Commercial pilots often begin their careers flying for air taxi companies or private businesses. These jobs require fewer hours of flight experience and less extensive testing than working for large airlines, and they allow pilots to master fairly simple aircraft before moving on to more sophisticated ones.

Most pilots employed by large airlines start as flight engineers. As they gain experience, they advance to copilot and then to captain. Promotions depend on seniority, and reaching captain may take anywhere from 5 to 15 years. Some captains eventually rise to management positions within the airlines. A college education that includes training in business and management is helpful for pilots who move out of the cockpit into such positions.

Other Careers in Aviation. Airlines offer a number of other jobs related to transporting people and goods by plane. Ticket agents issue airplane tickets, assign seats, and deal with the questions and problems of travelers. Flight attendants help passengers with seating, provide meal and beverage service, and carry out safety procedures. Baggage handlers load and unload luggage and cargo, and mechanics inspect and repair aircraft. Although such positions do not require a college education, they may require special skills and training.

Aviation-related jobs are also available with the government—most notably in air traffic control. Air traffic controllers are responsible for directing the movements of aircraft in the air and on the ground. They make sure that planes fly on approved routes, maintain a safe distance from each other, and do not interfere with the operation of other aircraft. They also coordinate the movement of aircraft on the ground at airports. Air traffic controllers often have college degrees. They are selected through a rigorous screening process organized by the FAA. Successful candidates then complete three to four months of intensive

The Air Force consists of many different units, called commands; these fighter pilots are training to fly attack planes.

training at the FAA's Aeronautical Center Academy in Oklahoma City. Traffic controllers must have a good memory and be able to make quick decisions while under great stress.

Aerospace

The aerospace industry is involved with the design, development, testing, and operation of commercial and military aircraft, missiles, and spacecraft. Although many people who work in the field are aerospace engineers, the industry also employs pilots, astronauts, and many other types of engineers.

The Aircraft Industry.

Most jobs in the aircraft industry deal with the design, manufacture, and repair of aircraft. People who design and build aircraft generally have college degrees in fields such as aerospace engineering or metallurgy, a branch of science dealing with metals. The workers who assemble aircraft need mechanical skills; most also receive extensive on-the-job and classroom training to keep up with changing technology. Aircraft mechanics often receive training by studying at technical and vocational schools or by working under experienced mechanics.

Aerospace Engineers.

Aerospace engineers develop new technologies for guidance and navigation systems, instruments and communications, fuels and **propulsion** systems, and weaponry. Most specialize in a particular area of study, such as mechanics, **aerodynamics,** propulsion, **thermodynamics,** or electronics.

Aerospace engineers must have advanced training in mathematics, physics, and fields of science related to their areas of interest and expertise. Most individuals earn at least a master's degree; many have doctoral degrees. Because technology changes so rapidly in this field, aerospace engineers need to update their knowledge constantly through continuing education.

Most aerospace engineers are employed by companies that design and build aircraft and aircraft parts, guided missiles, rockets, and spacecraft. In the United States a significant number work for government agencies such as the Department of Defense and the National Aeronautics and Space Administration (NASA). Many aerospace jobs are related to national defense and require extensive background checks, drug screening, and security clearance. Aerospace engineers also work for companies involved in communications, testing, and research.

Pilots and Astronauts.

A number of pilots work in the aerospace field, testing new or experimental aircraft. Test pilots must have the same qualifications as other pilots, and many also have college degrees in engineering. They monitor the performance of the aircraft they fly and offer suggestions to designers and engineers for improvements. Many test pilots received their flight training in the military.

A select group of individuals work for NASA as astronauts. They are divided into two groups: pilots and mission specialists. Pilot astronauts

propulsion *process of driving or propelling*

aerodynamics *branch of science that deals with the motion of air and the effects of such motion on planes and other objects*

thermodynamics *branch of science concerned with the relation between heat and mechanical energy*

control the spacecraft and command the mission. Mission specialists help maintain the spacecraft and its equipment and perform specialized tasks such as conducting experiments and launching satellites.

Individuals who want to become astronauts must have college degrees in science, mathematics, or engineering, as well as several years of related work experience. They must pass demanding physical tests. Those chosen as astronauts take a yearlong program that includes flight training, survival training, and classroom instruction in various sciences and medicine. They must learn how to operate spacecraft and perform various activities under spacelike conditions such as weightlessness. Candidates for pilot astronaut positions also need extensive flight experience.

Water Transportation

People with jobs related to water transportation operate, maintain, and manage ships, boats, barges, tugs, ferries, and shipping lines. Their work may take them far afield on the open seas or keep them fairly close to home in harbors and offices. Shipping company officials oversee the planning and coordination of freight and passenger service. At sea, pursers maintain the ship's records and financial accounts and assist passengers in many ways.

Captains, Pilots, and Officers. Captains are in command of ships and are responsible for overseeing the operation of their vessels and the work of the crew. They set the ship's course and speed, **maneuver** the vessel, and determine its position using navigational equipment. They give orders to crew members who steer the ship and run the engines, as well as to those in charge of communicating with other vessels and operating shipboard equipment. Captains also keep ship records, oversee the loading and unloading of cargo and passengers, and see that proper procedures and safety practices are followed.

Pilots guide ships in and out of harbors, on rivers, and in other situations where one must be familiar with local water depths, currents, tides, and hazards. Pilots on river and canal vessels generally are part of the regular crew, while harbor pilots often only accompany ships that are entering or leaving port. A harbormaster controls the use of the port and enforces safety regulations.

To become a captain or pilot, an individual often begins as a deck officer. Deck officers, or mates, oversee the ship's day-to-day operations and make sure that the captain's orders are carried out. Large ships carrying cargo overseas usually have a first mate, second mate, and third mate. Deck officers can rise in rank as they gain experience.

Another group of officers on ships are engineers. Engineering officers operate, maintain, and repair engines, pumps, and other machinery on ships. There are generally several ranks of engineer, including a chief engineer and various assistants.

Captains, deck officers, and engineers need licenses from the U.S. Coast Guard to operate specific types of vessels. Deck and engineering

Not Working 9 to 5

Although careers in transportation often provide an opportunity for travel, they may also involve unpredictable working hours. Many freight train crews, for example, do not have regular schedules. Workers put their names on a list, and when their turn comes, they are assigned to the next train. Long-haul truck drivers often travel through the night, when highway traffic is lighter. Even people who operate on fairly fixed schedules, such as airline pilots and flight attendants, often work all hours of the day or night and may spend several days at a time away from home.

maneuver to make a series of changes in course

This tugboat captain watches the oil tanker he is leading through the harbor of Sydney, Australia.

merchant marine *vessels engaged in commerce; officers and crews of such vessels*

nautical *relating to ships and sailors*

officers in the **merchant marine** must be graduates of a merchant marine academy, which provides schooling in **nautical** and marine sciences.

Seamen and Oilers. Seamen, or deckhands, operate vessels under the guidance of deck officers and help keep their ships in good condition. They stand watch, do maintenance work, load and unload cargo, and operate deck equipment such as lifeboats and anchors. Large vessels often have a head seaman called the boatswain.

Oilers work below deck under the supervision of a ship's engineering officers. They maintain and repair the machinery that powers the vessel. Oilers and seamen usually learn the necessary skills on the job. As they gain experience, they may take courses in seamanship and eventually qualify to become deck or engineering officers, pilots, and captains.

Travel and Tourism

People in the travel and tourism industry provide travelers with services before and during their trips. This includes providing travel information, planning trips, arranging reservations and tickets, and escorting tours.

Travel Agents. Travel agents help people make arrangements for trips. With direct access to the computerized reservation systems used by airlines and other passenger carriers, they can assist travelers in getting tickets and boarding passes. Their work ranges from simply providing information about flight times and availability to planning an entire business trip or vacation complete with transportation, accommodations, and sightseeing expeditions.

Travel agents may advise customers on tourist attractions, weather conditions, passport and visa requirements, currency exchange rates, and health hazards. They may visit the hotels and resorts they recommend to check on cleanliness, comfort, and service. Most agents have a college degree and training from a specialized program in tourism. Travel experience and some knowledge of foreign languages, computers, and business are helpful. Travel counselors who work for automobile clubs perform many of the same services as travel agents.

Travelers also obtain information from national, state, and local tourist offices. Representatives in these offices answer questions and provide material about an area's special attractions.

Tour Escorts. Tour escorts accompany groups of travelers on organized trips. They check hotel and transportation arrangements, oversee scheduling, and may act as guides. People who become tour escorts must be able to handle travel emergencies or problems quickly and calmly. They should also be knowledgeable about the places visited so that they can provide information and answer questions about local customs and laws. *See also* AIRLINE INDUSTRY; ASTRONAUTS; AUTOMOBILE INDUSTRY; AUTOMOBILES: RELATED INDUSTRIES; CRUISE SHIPS; DRIVING; LABOR UNIONS; MERCHANT MARINE; NAVIES; PILOTS, AIRCRAFT; RAILROAD INDUSTRY; RAILROAD WORKERS; SHIPPING INDUSTRY; SHIPS AND BOATS; TOURISM; TRAVEL INDUSTRY; TRUCKING INDUSTRY.

Cargo Ships

Cargo ships, or freighters, haul the goods and materials of commerce on lakes, rivers, and oceans. Traveling from harbor to harbor, they link the world's many ports and serve as the workhorses of the global shipping industry.

History of Cargo Ships

The first cargo vessels were probably the same rafts and canoes that carried people. Well before the beginning of history, people used boats to transport their belongings.

Ancient and Medieval Shipbuilding. The development of oars and, much later, sails increased the speed and distance that ships could travel. New methods of construction led to bigger boats. Canoes made from hollow tree trunks were limited in size, but boats built of wooden planks and animal skins could be as large as their builders could make them. As vessels became larger, the amount of cargo they could transport increased as well.

Some of the earliest seagoing boats were built by Minoans on the island of Crete around 5000 B.C., and about a thousand years later, Egyptians sailed ships made of planks along the Nile River. From 1000 to 250 B.C. the Phoenicians improved on Egyptian designs and the Greek historian Herodotus claimed that their trading ships sailed as far as the Indian Ocean. Later civilizations, including the Greeks, Romans, Norse, Arabs, and Chinese, built extensive trading empires across waters such as the Mediterranean Sea and Indian Ocean. Their ships carried all sorts of cargo, from Lebanese cedar to Indian tea.

During the Middle Ages, European shipbuilders made remarkable advances in sail design and deck construction. Sails replaced oars in all large European vessels except those used in the Mediterranean. By the 1500s large ships with multiple masts, decks, and sails made routine crossings of the Atlantic Ocean. In the following centuries, the ships of European empires sailed around the world just as regularly, bringing about a truly global commerce. However, the basic design of cargo ships remained the same for hundreds of years.

Modern Innovations. The industrial revolution of the late 1700s led to dramatic changes in shipbuilding during the 1800s. Sails gave way to steam engines, and iron began to replace wood as a building material. The invention of steel, stronger and lighter than iron, led to even larger and faster ships. By the early 1900s heavy oil engines and diesel engines were introduced; diesel engines still power most large ships. Very big and fast, modern cargo ships can carry 17 times the amount of cargo of freighters from World War II in the same period of time.

Types of Cargo Ships

Cargo ships are classified as cargo liners and tramp carriers. Run by large shipping companies, cargo liners operate on fixed schedules along regular routes. Tramps, generally the property of smaller companies and ship owners, will make single voyages to any port. Both liners and tramps can be divided according to cargo. General cargo ships carry a variety of materials and goods; tankers transport liquids such as oil; and dry bulk carriers haul loose solids such as grain.

General Cargo Ships. General cargo ships, the most basic freighters, have large cargo areas called holds beneath the deck. An electric crane is used to load cargo into the holds. A single structure, known

Loaded with containers, this cargo ship heads into harbor in Vancouver, Canada, guided by a tugboat.

as an island, rises from the deck at the rear of the ship. It contains the ship's bridge and living quarters.

Since the 1950s, the most important innovation in cargo shipping has been the development of the container ship. On a standard cargo ship, many workers are needed to pack goods of all different shapes and sizes into the holds. A container ship is built to carry a certain number of standard-sized containers that arrive at the docks already packed. Most containers measure 8 feet (2.4 m) high, 8 feet (2.4 m) wide, and from 20 to 40 feet (6 to 12 m) long. Crane operators and deckhands can load and unload the containers easily, saving time, space, effort, and money. Another recent form of general cargo ship is the roll-on/roll-off vessel. In this arrangement, containers mounted on wheels simply drive up ramps and into the hold. Cargo such as cars and trucks are also easily loaded onto and carried by roll-on/roll-off ships.

Tankers. Tankers were among the earliest specialty vessels—ships designed to transport a specific kind of cargo, petroleum. In 1878 a shipper named Ludwig Nobel realized that instead of filling barrels with oil and then loading them onto a ship, he could have his vessel serve as a giant oil tank. Modern tankers have several chambers inside, to reduce the amount spilled in case of a break in the hull. Most tankers continue to carry petroleum, although they also carry other liquids such as liquefied natural gas.

Like all cargo ships, tankers have increased tremendously in size so that more cargo can be shipped for the cost of a single voyage. The largest "supertankers" measure more than 1,500 feet (460 m) in length and carry 500,000 tons of oil. However, some critics consider them dangerous because they have difficulty maneuvering in shallow or narrow waters, and a single spill can create a major environmental disaster.

Dry Bulk Carriers and Other Cargo Ships. Dry bulk carriers are similar to tankers, but their chambers are filled with loose, solid cargo such as grain, coal, or iron ore. Although hoses and pumps can drain a tanker, powerful scoops, carts, and suction machines are needed to unload dry bulk. Multipurpose ships have different sections for general cargo, liquids, and dry bulk. Barges are raftlike cargo vessels; those without engines are pulled by tugboats. Lighter aboard ship (LASH) vehicles are designed to carry lighters—a type of barge—on their decks. When the ship reaches port, the barges are lowered into the water and towed upriver by tugboats. Tugboats also play an important role in guiding large cargo ships on rivers and in harbors. *See also* BARGES; CONTAINERIZATION; HARBORS AND PORTS; SHIPS AND BOATS, TYPES OF; TANKERS.

Waves of War

During World War II, the United States mounted massive shipping efforts to keep its forces around the world supplied with food, uniforms, weapons, ammunition, and new recruits. American shipbuilders produced more than 3,000 Liberty and Victory cargo ships. They achieved this amazing feat in part by following an important principle of mass production: all the cargo ships were built from the same standard designs. Parts could be made and fitted with great speed and regularity. With holds full of men and machines, these sturdy vessels were vital to the U.S. war effort.

Carrier Pigeons   *see Delivery Services.*

Cartography   *see Maps and Charts.*

Carts, Carriages, and Wagons

What's in the Name?

The names of some carts and carriages contain clues to their origins or tell us something about what they were like. For example, the jinricksha originated in Japan, and in Japanese its name means "human-powered vehicle." The word *coach* came from the town of Kotze, Hungary, where vehicles of this type originated. The bespattered appearance of passenger wagons earned them the nickname *mud wagons*. The sociable was a passenger wagon with two rows of seating facing each other, an arrangement that promoted friendly exchanges. Just the opposite was the sulky, a light cart built for just one person—perhaps favored by sulking individuals.

suspension system of springs and other parts that supports the body of a vehicle on the axles

Since the invention of the wheel around 3500 B.C., humans have developed an astounding variety of wheeled vehicles to carry themselves and their goods. Two-wheeled vehicles pulled by animals are considered carts; those with four or more wheels are carriages, which carry passengers, or wagons, basically used for cargo. Carts, carriages, and wagons were the only land vehicles for thousands of years, and they are still used in many forms.

The First Wheeled Vehicles. The earliest known cargo vehicles were sledges—flat, sledlike platforms hauled across the ground by people or animals. The Sumerians of what is now Iraq were probably the first to fasten wheels to sledges. They may have been using primitive two-wheeled carts by around 3000 B.C. or even earlier.

The cart originated in the Middle East but spread to other areas, such as northern India and central Asia, by 2500 B.C. Over the next 1,200 years they gradually appeared in Greece, Egypt, China, and northern Europe. Ancient artworks contain many images of a particular type of cart: the war or hunting chariot pulled by a single animal or a team. Early chariots had two wheels, but a four-wheeled version came later.

The four-wheeled wagon developed more slowly than the cart because it was difficult to steer. Then the Romans introduced a wagon with a front axle that could pivot from side to side. This steerable wagon—essentially a wooden box on wheels—was in wide use by the 100s B.C. From this basic wagon came many forms of passenger vehicles, known as coaches and carriages, that appeared in later centuries.

The Roman Era and the Middle Ages. The Romans were skilled and energetic road builders. They also developed new types of carts and carriages by adapting and improving the designs of vehicles from countries they added to their far-flung empire. Vehicle traffic was common in Roman territories. After about A.D. 500, as Roman power declined, the state of transportation in Europe went downhill as well. Roads fell into disrepair and disuse. Chronicles from the early Middle Ages contain few mentions of carriages, although people continued to make and use crude carts and wagons.

Carriage building surged again in the late Middle Ages, and references to carriages are common in literature and other historical sources from the 1100s and later. But passengers traveling on Europe's rough roads experienced severe shaking and jolting. Carriage makers attempted to cushion the shocks by hanging the compartment from chains. By the 1300s they were using leather straps for **suspension.** Although these devices did not guarantee passengers an entirely smooth ride, given the poor state of roads, any improvement was a blessing.

During the 1400s and 1500s, stage wagons appeared in England and Europe. These were long, heavy wagons that carried passengers and freight over set routes, with a wagon and team for each stage of the route. Another important development in the 1500s was the appearance of the first coaches in Hungary. The roofed passenger compartment of the coach featured side doors or curtains and was mounted on a suspension system. In the centuries that followed, the term *coach* came to be used for a closed carriage built to hold four people on two facing seats, with the driver on a separate seat in front of the passenger cabin.

The Golden Age of Coaches and Carriages.

The period from the early 1600s to the early 1900s was the high point in the history of coaches and carriages, both in the total number of vehicles in use and in the variety of designs.

Several important advances made carriages easier to use and more comfortable for passengers. Builders began making the front wheels smaller than the rear wheels, which allowed the front axle to turn sharply without grinding the wheels against the wagon or carriage body. During the 1700s carriage makers introduced metal springs as a replacement for the leather straps used as suspension systems. In 1804 Obadiah Elliot, an English coach maker, invented the elliptical spring, a new kind of metal suspension that was much lighter than the earlier version. This technology, combined with the new method of surfacing roads with **macadam** for greater smoothness, made passenger travel far more comfortable than it had ever been.

A great many types of carriages came into use, but names for the same kind of vehicles varied from place to place. Among the more common varieties were the cabriolet, a two-wheeled carriage from Italy (four-wheeled versions appeared later). Cabriolets were widely used as vehicles for hire in France, and the word *cab* eventually came to mean any hired cart or carriage. A hired coach might also be called a hack, or a hackney cab.

macadam *small stones bound together with tar or asphalt*

Wheeled vehicles have been used for almost 5,000 years to transport people and cargo. Here, a man in Thailand drives a cart pulled by oxen.

Children's Wagons

Throughout the ages children have played with small, simple versions of the basic wagon, with handles for pulling instead of the shafts to which draft animals are attached. Most early wagons were handcrafted from wood. Antonio Pasin, creator of the famous Radio Flyer wagon, launched his business in 1923, producing wooden vehicles for children. After a few years he began using metal stamping, borrowed from the auto industry, to make his wagons. The Radio Flyer model soared to popularity in the 1930s. In later models the company added working headlights, fenders, and streamlined design, adapted from modern cars and trains.

In the United States the two-wheeled cabriolet was sometimes called a buggy, though that term often applied to a lightweight four-wheeled carriage for one or two passengers, with a folding top. A chair or sulky was a light open passenger cart, usually for one passenger; a chaise was a two-passenger cart with a folding top. A chariot resembled a coach but had only one seat and held one or two passengers.

Larger vehicles included the landau, a solidly built vehicle that contained two facing seats. Instead of a closed passenger compartment, it had two folding tops that met in the middle. A barouche was a carriage for four to six passengers, with a folding top over the rear seat. The term *phaeton* referred to a variety of four-wheeled carriages with folding tops. Unlike the coach or landau, the phaeton did not have a separate seat for the driver and was often driven by its owner. A more workaday vehicle was the spring wagon, which had seats that could be removed to make room for freight.

Wagon and carriage makers in the United States produced a number of vehicles suited to the rough terrain of the new country. These included lightweight stages with little suspension for use when speed was more important than comfort—such as for carrying mail rather than passengers. One of the most famous American vehicles was the Conestoga wagon, a sturdy, canvas-topped vehicle designed for hauling cargo over mountain roads. Many pioneers traveled westward in a later version of the Conestoga wagon known as the prairie schooner because its canvas cover looked like sails. The Conestoga was used mostly in Pennsylvania and Ohio; the prairie schooner carried people from the Middle West across the mountains and plains of the West. Another horse-drawn vehicle, the Concord coach, was built in New Hampshire in the early 1800s. It was widely used for stagecoach service between eastern cities and the West.

Uses of Carts and Carriages. The cart, a most ancient form of transport, is still in use today in such forms as the wheelbarrow, the donkey cart, and the bicycle cart. The jinricksha, also called the ricksha or rickshaw, was a passenger cart pulled by a runner. Appearing in Japan in the late 1800s, it soon spread to many Asian cities. The pedicab, a passenger cart like a tricycle with a rider instead of a runner as the power source, replaced the jinricksha but later gave way to motorized two-person cabs.

The first scheduled mail, cargo, and passenger transport services used carriages. Starting around 1600, stagecoaches provided long-distance transportation in Europe during a time when few people had their own means of travel. Stagecoach lines were organized in the American colonies in the 1750s. In the mid-1800s organizers of public sightseeing tours in England introduced long passenger wagons called *char-à-bancs* (cart with benches)—the ancestors of modern tour buses.

Carriage manufacturing reached its peak in the early 1900s, but already the automobile was casting a shadow over the roads of industrialized nations. Farmers and merchants in many developing nations still use carts and carriages on an everyday basis, but trains and buses have taken over most passenger transport in these areas. *See also* ANIMALS, PACK AND DRAFT; CHARIOTS; CONESTOGA WAGONS; STAGECOACHES; WHEELS.

Catamarans

A catamaran is a boat with more than one hull. Although the catamaran's basic design is ancient, modern boatbuilders have developed improved models for racing, recreation, and public transport.

Catamaran means "tied logs" in the Tamil language of India and Sri Lanka, where for centuries people made raftlike boats by lashing together two or more logs or dugout canoes. Pacific Islanders and the inhabitants of the western coast of South America built similar vessels. Propelled by many paddlers and sailors, these early catamarans could complete voyages of more than 2,000 miles (3,220 km) between island groups in the Pacific Ocean.

In the late 1800s designers began experimenting with twin-hulled racing sailing craft and found that they were generally faster than single-hulled boats. In fact, catamarans proved to be so much faster that the sailing organizations of the time banned them from races. Today there are special races for catamarans. The main disadvantage of the catamaran is that if it flips over it will not turn right side up again. Catamaran design is also being used in ferries and in military vessels. *See also* Canoes and Kayaks; Rafts.

Cattle Trails

Cattle trails belong to both the history and the mythology of the North American West. In the late 1800s the trails were avenues for the transport of large herds of livestock, and they contributed to the growth of a profitable new commerce. At the same time, the long, demanding cattle drives over these trails earned cowboys a lasting place in songs, stories, and legends.

Early Livestock Drives. By the mid-1500s the Spanish, the first ranchers in North America, were driving herds of cattle north from their colony in Mexico into the borderlands of Texas and the Southwest. These drives introduced the long-horned cattle that became the typical livestock of Texas and the West. During the 1700s and early 1800s, Spanish settlers in Texas drove both horses and cattle east to markets in New Orleans.

Livestock driving occurred elsewhere during this period—whenever and wherever people needed to move animals over long distances. However, for the ranchers and cowboys of Texas, cattle driving became a way of life. Before 1836, while Texas still belonged to Mexico, Texans moved their livestock along a "Beef Trail" to New Orleans. Later, in the 1840s and 1850s, they drove herds of longhorns to Missouri and Chicago. Some of the oxen that went to Missouri ended up pulling freight wagons and settlers' wagons over the trails to Oregon and California. By the mid-1860s the eastward cattle trails were closed by increased settlement in Missouri and the Midwest.

The Golden Age of Cattle Trails. After the Civil War, the railroads began pushing west through Kansas. A livestock shipper from Illinois named John G. McCoy realized that trains offered the perfect link between Texas cattle and Northeastern markets. In 1867 McCoy opened a cattle market in Abilene, Kansas, a small town on the Kansas

Frederic Remington's engraving from the late 1800s captures the spirit of life on the cattle trails. It shows cowboys driving their herds across the plains to be sold at market.

The Not-So-Wild West?

Dodge City, Kansas, and other cow towns at the ends of the cattle trails had plenty of saloons, gambling dens, and other rowdy establishments where cowboys could spend their hard-earned pay. Stories about these towns bristle with gunfighters and lawmen, brawls and shootouts. But the cow towns of the Old West may not have been as wild and blood-stained as they appear in most movies and fiction. Historical records show only 45 violent deaths in all the towns between 1870 and 1885, the peak of the cattle-drive era.

Pacific rail line. Texas ranchers, who had been looking for a better way to get their cattle to market, drove their herds to Abilene. That year 7,000 head passed through this livestock center on their way to the stockyards of Chicago; four years later, the number reached 600,000.

Many of the herds sent north from Texas to meet the railroads followed the Chisholm Trail. This famous and heavily used route ran from southern to northern Texas, picking up cattle from smaller trails along the way, and then crossed the Indian Territory (now Oklahoma) and entered Kansas. Another route, the Goodnight-Loving Trail, led west and north into New Mexico and Colorado. As the railroads extended westward, the cowboys created new trails. At the ends of these trails were "cow towns" such as Newton, Caldwell, and Wichita in Kansas, which all had rail connections to the East.

Not all the cattle driven up from Texas went straight to market. Many ranchers led their cattle to the unfenced northern plains of Montana, Wyoming, the Dakotas, and even southern Canada to graze and breed. But in the late 1880s, a flood of settlers and some very severe winters greatly reduced open-range ranching. In the following years, settlers, fences, and more local rail lines brought an end to cattle driving even in Texas.

Life on the Trail Drives. The large-scale movement of livestock reached a peak in the late 1860s and the 1870s, with some herds numbering as many as 4,000 cattle. A drive usually lasted for two or three months and could cover 1,000 miles (1,610 km), requiring careful planning and good timing. It also required superb horses and horsemanship. The trail boss and the cowboys who worked for him had to make sure that the cattle got water every few days and had time to graze. They also had to control the cattle, preventing jittery animals from panicking and stampeding as they crossed streams, endured thunderstorms, or faced Indian attacks. Herders looked for cattle trails that offered smooth terrain, water sources, and grass for the animals. *See also* ANIMALS, PACK AND DRAFT; HORSES.

Challenger Disaster

NASA *National Aeronautics and Space Administration, the U.S. space agency*

On January 28, 1986, 9 miles (14 km) above the Earth, the U.S. space shuttle *Challenger* burst into flames and broke into pieces. The sudden explosion shocked the spectators on the ground and millions of television viewers worldwide. The investigation that followed revealed that serious flaws in design and judgment had led to the deaths of the seven people on board.

Concerns Before Liftoff. The two solid rocket boosters (SRBs) of a space shuttle are constructed in sections held together by large rubber rings called O-rings. When the solid fuel ignites, the rockets expand, and the O-rings swell to keep a tight seal.

As **NASA** prepared *Challenger* for its tenth mission, engineers at Morton Thiokol—the company that had built the shuttle's two SRBs—expressed serious concerns about safety. On several flights, O-rings had been damaged and charred by burning fuel, especially at low temperatures. On that morning, engineers worried that the unusually cold weather would make the rings less flexible, risking serious problems.

However, several issues overrode the safety concerns. Other companies were competing to build the boosters, and executives at Morton Thiokol did not want to disappoint NASA by seeming too cautious. NASA officials were also impatient to launch the shuttle and keep to their ambitious schedule of 15 flights that year.

Launch and Failure. While the officials argued, 3-foot (1-m) icicles hung from *Challenger*'s launch tower. Inside the crew cabin waited six astronauts—mission commander Francis R. "Dick" Scobee, pilot Michael J. Smith, Ronald McNair, Ellison Onizuka, Judith Resnick, and Gregory Jarvis. Also aboard was Christa McAuliffe, a high school teacher from New Hampshire. She had planned to teach two lessons to classrooms around the country while in space.

Later in the morning, the sun emerged and melted the icicles. NASA decided to proceed with the launch. As the shuttle's main engines and the SRBs fired and *Challenger* lifted off, the O-rings were slow to expand. A puff of black smoke appeared on the right booster. The O-ring then completed the seal, but it was weakened. Fifty-nine seconds into the flight, as *Challenger* soared into the upper atmosphere at about twice the speed of sound, the seal gave way and burning fuel flared out.

The fire burned holes in the SRB and a support that held the rocket to the external fuel tank. Less than two minutes after liftoff the strut burned through, allowing the booster to swing around, punch a hole in the tank, and ignite the fuel. The tank and **orbiter** disintegrated, and the crew died within seconds as their air supply was cut off.

orbiter *piloted section of a space shuttle that goes into space*

The Aftermath. Images of the disaster raced around the world, replayed on television screens everywhere. As Americans mourned the loss of life and absorbed the blow to their national pride, a special commission investigated the accident. Its final report laid the blame on NASA and Morton Thiokol for their overconfidence and their failure to place safety before scheduling and politics.

NASA grounded the remaining shuttles for 32 months while it improved their design and established better safety procedures. The shuttle flight program resumed on September 29, 1988, with the successful launch of the redesigned shuttle *Discovery*. *See also* ACCIDENTS; ASTRONAUTS; SPACE SHUTTLES.

Channel Tunnel

The Channel Tunnel, also known as the Chunnel, allows railway cars to travel between Britain and France under the English Channel. Its opening provided passengers and freight shippers with a high-speed rail route, protected from the weather conditions faced by boats traveling on the open sea.

The idea of creating a tunnel under the Channel was proposed several times in the 1800s. French mining engineer Albert Mathieu prepared plans for an underground passage in 1802, but it was never built. Eighty years later another attempt was organized and work began. Crews dug more than 6,000 feet (1,830 m) from the English side before an outcry in Britain over the chance of a foreign invasion through the tunnel brought the project to a halt.

In 1963 the idea for a Channel tunnel emerged again. This time Britain and France formed a joint commission to carry out surveys and studies. Ten years later the two countries agreed to go forward and construction began. In 1975, with more than 1 mile (1.6 km) of excavation completed at each end, economic problems led to cancellation of the project.

Work on the tunnel resumed in 1987. This time it proceeded steadily, with crews digging from both sides of the Channel. Builders used state-of-the-art technology, including enormous tunnel-boring machines and lasers, which guided the excavation with pinpoint accuracy. As the digging machines advanced, conveyor belts cleared away mounds of debris. By the time the tunnel was ready to open, workers had moved more than 17 million tons of dirt and stone.

Completed in 1994 at a cost of more than $12 billion, the Channel Tunnel is one of the largest engineering projects in history. It extends for 31 miles (50 km) between Folkstone, England, and Calais, France, at

The Channel Tunnel, 31 miles (50 km) in length, consists of three tunnels between the French and English coasts: two main rail tunnels and one smaller service tunnel.

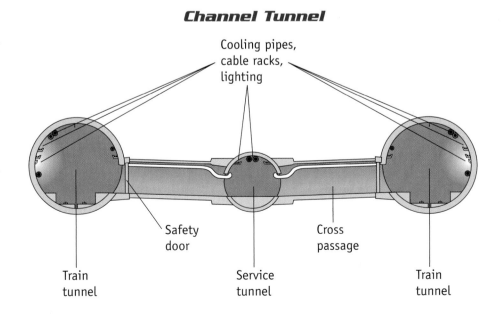

Channel Tunnel

Cooling pipes, cable racks, lighting

Safety door

Cross passage

Train tunnel

Service tunnel

Train tunnel

depths of between 81 feet (25 m) and 132 feet (40 m) under the seabed. It consists of three tunnels. Two rail tunnels, one in each direction, serve trains carrying passengers, vehicles, and freight. A smaller service tunnel between the two main tunnels is used for maintenance work and emergency access. Passageways every 1,200 feet (370 m) connect the service tunnel with the rail tunnels.

The three tunnels are constructed of concrete with a layer of cast iron for added strength. Air ducts release the gusts of air forced through the tunnels by high-speed trains. Massive coolers at both ends keep the passages from becoming too hot.

Electric trains move through the Chunnel at speeds of up to 80 miles an hour (129 km per hour). The underground trip between the British and French coasts takes about 35 minutes, less than half the time of a ferry voyage across the English Channel. Passengers on one of the most popular routes—between London and Paris—reach their destinations in only three hours. *See also* TUNNELS.

Chariots

The people of ancient cultures from China, Greece, and Rome used chariots for activities such as hunting, racing, and warfare. This print, inspired by a Greek vase painting, depicts a young man leaving for athletic games.

A chariot is a two- or four-wheeled open passenger cart pulled by draft animals. Among the earliest vehicles known, chariots were used in various ancient cultures for processions, recreation, and war.

The first chariots appeared in the Middle East, in the region that is now Iraq, between 3000 and 2000 B.C. They were heavy, four-wheeled wagons with solid wood wheels, pulled by teams of oxen or onagers—a type of wild ass.

Between 2000 and 1500 B.C. a two-wheeled form of the chariot emerged. Lighter wheels consisting of rims and spokes replaced the solid, heavy wheels used earlier. Easier to steer than the four-wheeled version, this vehicle spread quickly across the ancient world. At around the same time people began using horses as draft animals. The combination of the horse's strength and speed, the spoked wheel, and the two-wheeled design made the chariot into a fast, effective military vehicle. Chariots used in battle carried a driver and a warrior, who probably dismounted from the chariot to fight.

By 1400 B.C. people from China to Greece used chariots. The typical war chariot consisted of a wooden platform mounted above an axle and two wheels, with a pole extending forward to which the animals could be harnessed. Side screens and a wooden or leather front dashboard gave the riders some protection. Sometimes sharp blades were attached to the hubs of the wheels to slice at enemies or their horses as the chariot rumbled along. The chariots of royalty might be decorated with fine materials such as ivory, silver, and gold. These handsome vehicles appeared in processions and were sometimes buried with their owners.

By the 300s B.C. the Greeks and Romans had abandoned the war chariot in favor of cavalry, or soldiers mounted on horseback. Chariots remained in use, however, particularly in sport. Chariot racing was the opening event at the Olympic Games in Greece. Similar competitions took place in Rome, where spectators bet on their favorite chariot teams and successful drivers became celebrities. *See also* ANIMALS, PACK AND DRAFT; CARTS, CARRIAGES, AND WAGONS; HORSES.

Charts

see Maps and Charts.

Chevrolet

Chevrolet is the brand name of various models of cars and trucks produced by the General Motors Corporation, the largest automaker in the world. Chevrolets are among the most popular American-made motor vehicles.

The early Chevrolet models were produced by the Chevrolet Motor Car Company, a firm established in Detroit in 1911 by William Durant and Louis Chevrolet. Chevrolet, an auto racer and designer, left after a few years, but the company continued under his name.

The first Chevrolet car, the 1912 Classic Six, had a powerful six-cylinder engine, but the model cost more than $2,000 and did not sell well. Durant reorganized the company the following year, building an assembly plant in New York in addition to the manufacturing operations in Michigan.

In 1914 Chevrolet introduced two low-priced models, the Baby Grand touring car and the Royal Mail roadster. Nearly 16,000 of these cars were sold over the next two years, and Chevrolet became a leading name in automobile manufacturing. In 1915 the company produced the 490 model that sold for $490, priced to compete with Ford's Model T.

The Chevrolet Motor Car Company was acquired by General Motors (GM) in 1916 but remained a separate division. Chevrolet automobiles have been manufactured by GM ever since. GM used its Chevrolet line to offer good, low-cost cars, such as the 1928 sedan that outsold the Ford Model T. Between the late 1920s and the 1970s, Chevrolets were generally top sellers. Other popular models have included the classic Corvette sports car and the family-sized Suburban. *See also* AUTOMOBILE INDUSTRY; AUTOMOBILES; AUTOMOBILES, HISTORY OF; ENGINES; SPORTS CARS; TRUCKS.

China Trade

Trade between China and the Western world dates back to the Middle Ages. After Italian explorer Marco Polo traveled to China in the 1270s, he wrote an account of the exotic lands he visited and the riches he saw. His book inspired European merchants to set up trading links with Asia.

Trade with China also played a significant role in the early history of the United States. After the Revolutionary War, Britain prohibited American vessels from entering the ports of Britain and its colonies. Moreover, the British, French, and Dutch had **monopolies** on many of the richest markets in Asia. The United States badly needed new trade.

In the 1780s American merchants sought opportunities in China, which was not yet dominated by the European powers. The Chinese emperor had opened only one port to foreigners—Canton (now known as Guangzhou). Soon trading ships from New York, Philadelphia, Boston, Baltimore, and other cities were sailing around Africa and east across the Indian Ocean to China.

Americans learned that the Chinese were eager to obtain furs. They responded by setting up a three-cornered trade route. Merchants on the

monopoly control of a market or product by a single company or country

Atlantic coast carried clothing, hardware, and other manufactured goods around South America to the Pacific Northwest. There, settlers bought the goods and gave the merchants otter and beaver pelts in return. The trading ships crossed the Pacific Ocean with the furs and came home with their holds full of Chinese goods, including tea, silk, and porcelain. These fetched high prices in American cities on the East Coast.

The China trade expanded in 1844, when China agreed to a treaty with the United States that opened additional ports to Americans. By then, however, Americans had regained access to British markets and trade with China was no longer as important. *See also* TRADE AND COMMERCE.

Chrysler Corporation

see Automobile Industry.

Circumnavigation

A circumnavigation is a trip around something, such as an island or a continent. But the word most often refers to a journey around the Earth, an enterprise that has occupied a special place in the history of transportation—as well as in the public imagination. Many circumnavigators were explorers who brought back surprising and valuable geographic discoveries. Others were pioneers who hoped to prove the worthiness of a particular kind of transportation.

The Great Explorers. Ferdinand Magellan, a Portuguese navigator in the service of Spain, led the first expedition that sailed around the world. Magellan died on the way, but his lieutenant Juan Sebastián de Elcano completed the journey in 1522. This first circumnavigation had enormous importance, for it proved that all the oceans are connected, and it opened the vast Pacific Ocean to European seafarers.

Other mariners followed in Magellan's wake. Sir Francis Drake of England led the second global circumnavigation. He left England in 1577 with five ships and 166 men and returned in 1580 with one ship and 57 men—as well as a fortune in looted Spanish treasure. Drake's countryman Thomas Cavendish made the journey a few years later, followed by William Dampier, a pirate whose books about his three circumnavigations awakened Europe's interest in the Pacific.

The 1700s and 1800s brought the glory days of scientific exploration. Sea captains made round-the-world voyages for Britain, France, Spain, and Italy, putting whole nations and island chains onto European maps. Three Russian expeditions circumnavigated between 1803 and 1829. The first American to lead such a journey was Charles Wilkes of the U.S. Navy, who explored Antarctica and the South Pacific from 1838 to 1842.

Airplanes, Speed Records, and Stunts. In the days of Magellan and Drake, a voyage around the world inspired fear, awe, and courage, but by 1900 it had become a fairly commonplace event.

Ferdinand Magellan led the first expedition to sail completely around the globe. His route around the southern tip of South America passed through a treacherous waterway now called the Strait of Magellan.

Yet some of the old heroism returned when aviation pioneers dared to circle the globe in their noisy new contraptions.

In 1929 the German airship *Graf Zeppelin* circumnavigated in 21 days. The American airplane pilot Wiley Post became the first person to fly around the world alone in 1933, setting a new speed record of just under eight days. Five years later American industrialist Howard Hughes made the trip in a commercial airliner in less than four days. In the modern age of space flight, space shuttles and satellites circle the planet in just a few hours.

Though the speed races are over, people still seek adventure and publicity with circumnavigations that push the limits of transportation science and human endurance. In the late 1990s, several adventurers competed to be the first to circle the world in hot-air balloons, rowboats, and open-cockpit biplanes. They often enhanced their simple vehicles with the most advanced materials and electronic equipment. *See also* BALLOONS; EXPLORATION.

Civil Aeronautics Board

deregulation *process of removing restrictions and regulations*

The Civil Aeronautics Board (CAB) was an agency of the U.S. government responsible for regulating competition among airlines and promoting commercial air transportation. Until the **deregulation** of the airline industry in October 1978, the CAB had complete control over decisions about airline routes, fares, and the licensing of new airlines.

Before the creation of the CAB, the Commerce Department oversaw aviation safety and operations in the United States. In 1938 Congress passed the Civil Aeronautics Act, which established the Civil Aeronautics Authority. The organization (which became known as the CAB in 1940) had the authority to award routes to air carriers, set prices, and ensure safe operating practices. In 1958 responsibility for air safety was transferred to the newly established Federal Aviation Agency (now the Federal Aviation Administration).

The CAB closely controlled competition in the airline industry by limiting the number of new air carriers entering the market. Between 1938 and 1975, the board rejected nearly 100 petitions for new service. It also reviewed and usually denied the applications of existing airlines for new routes. Requests for routes were granted only after lengthy hearings in which the carrier had to prove that the new service would benefit the public and not cause financial harm to other airlines. In addition, the CAB made it almost impossible for airlines to offer discounted fares. These policies were designed to enable existing airlines to operate profitably.

During the 1970s, airline traffic grew dramatically, and new technology lowered operating costs. Politicians and the public protested that ticket prices were artificially high and did not reflect the actual cost of doing business.

In 1975 the CAB began to allow airlines to begin or end service on selected routes without its prior approval. Three years later the Airline Deregulation Act made this policy into law and gave airlines more flexibility in setting ticket prices. Finally, in 1984, the CAB was abolished, and its remaining duties—regulating airline mergers and handling complaints against airlines—were transferred to the U.S. Department of Transportation. *See also* AIRLINE INDUSTRY; FAA (FEDERAL AVIATION ADMINISTRATION); GOVERNMENT AND TRANSPORTATION; INTERSTATE COMMERCE COMMISSION; POSTAL SERVICE; REGULATION OF TRANSPORTATION; TRANSPORTATION, U.S. DEPARTMENT OF.

Classic Cars

see Vintage Cars.

Clipper Ships

Designed for maximum speed, clipper ships dominated maritime trade in the mid-1800s. Their name may have come from the way they clipped days and weeks from normal shipping times or from the speedy clip at which they traveled.

The first true clipper ship was designed by John W. Griffiths of New York in 1845. Called the *Rainbow,* it set the standard for clippers with a long, narrow hull, a deep stern, and a high angled bow. Unlike earlier vessels that rode the waves on round bottoms, clippers sliced through the swells. This design left limited space for cargo, but the clippers were built for speed.

The ship's three masts, nearly 200 feet (61 m) high, raised an astonishing spread of sails to catch any and all wind at sea. Some clippers even had masts tilted backward, braced against the enormous force the sails could harness. Captains needed large, well-trained crews to avoid breaking a mast while shifting the sails in a powerful gust.

The clipper was best suited for carrying small, highly profitable cargo that required quick delivery. As part of the era's China Trade, clippers transported manufactured goods from the Atlantic coast to settlers and gold miners in California. Captains competed to make the fastest trip from the Northeast around South America's Cape Horn to the West Coast. Boston shipbuilder Donald McKay's *Flying Cloud* set a record by completing the journey from New York to San Francisco in 89 days. From California, the vessels brought gold back to the Atlantic coast or headed for China to pick up tea, which fetched the highest prices if it reached the market while still fresh.

The clipper ship Flying Cloud, built in 1851, set a record when it sailed from New York to San Francisco in 89 days.

In 1849 the British lifted restrictions that had prevented foreign vessels from trading in their ports. American clippers began plying the Atlantic in greater numbers, among them McKay's *James Baines,* which crossed from Boston to Liverpool in just 12 days and 6 hours. But speed gradually became less important to merchants than the need to reduce shipping costs. They began to favor vessels called medium clippers that sacrificed sails for smaller crews.

When the Civil War curbed American commerce in the early 1860s, the British stepped up their production of ships. They built the finest of the late clippers, which were put to use in the tea trade with Asia. Then in 1869 the Suez Canal opened, linking the Mediterranean and the Red Seas and greatly shortening the sea route to Asia. Speed became less important to traders, and they turned to ships with greater cargo capacity. At the same time, large steamships that could match the clippers' pace appeared, and the era of sailing ships drew to a close. *See also* CHINA TRADE; SAILBOATS AND SAILING SHIPS; SHIPBUILDING; SUEZ CANAL.

Coaches

see Carts, Carriages, and Wagons; Stagecoaches.

Coast Guard

A coast guard is an agency responsible for marine safety and the enforcement of national **maritime** laws. Almost all countries with seacoasts have a coast guard. The United States Coast Guard, a branch of the armed services with 40,000 men and women, is notable for its size and the wide range of its responsibilities.

Formation of the Coast Guard. In 1790 Congress assigned ten armed sailing ships called cutters to enforce the nation's **customs** laws and to stop smuggling and piracy. This force, known first as the Revenue Marine and later as the Revenue Cutter Service, served under the Department of the Treasury.

In 1878 Congress created the Lifesaving Service, an agency responsible for helping ships and seafarers in distress. Because this agency often worked with the Revenue Cutter Service, the two merged in 1915 to form the U.S. Coast Guard. The guard also absorbed the Lighthouse Service and the Bureau of Marine Inspection and Navigation in 1939 and 1942, creating a single agency responsible for all maritime affairs not controlled by the U.S. Navy.

The Coast Guard became part of the Department of Transportation in 1967. It is divided into 12 regional districts with a central headquarters in Washington, D.C. Each district has a fleet of small boats and larger rescue ships, as well as helicopters and other aircraft. The Coast Guard Reserve enters active duty in times of emergency, and the Coast Guard Auxiliary assists with educational programs and other activities.

Role of the Coast Guard. The U.S. Coast Guard has numerous responsibilities. As a law enforcement agency, it is charged with overseeing all maritime laws related to shipping and navigation, including laws concerning recreational boating and safety. It also assists other agencies in policing customs, immigration, and environmental laws along the nation's shores and in preventing illegal drug traffic.

The Coast Guard regulates ships and equipment, conducts inspections, monitors the loading and unloading of cargo, and issues licenses for captains and

maritime related to the sea or shipping

customs tax on imported goods

The U.S. Coast Guard is responsible for ensuring safety at sea by enforcing maritime laws and investigating accidents.

crews of merchant vessels and passenger liners. In addition, the agency maintains various aids to navigation, such as lighthouses, buoys, fog signals, and radar stations. It also carries out activities related to safety, including educational programs on recreational boating and investigations into maritime accidents. Other responsibilities of the Coast Guard involve clearing ice from frozen waterways, locating and tracking icebergs, and collecting scientific data.

Search and rescue operations form another major part of the Coast Guard's duties. Its cutters, helicopters, and airplanes patrol shores and waterways, ready to assist vessels and sailors in distress. These missions often take the guard far into international ocean waters. In times of war, the Coast Guard comes under the authority of the U.S. Navy. Its officers, ships, and aircraft assist in tasks such as escorting naval vessels and transporting troops and supplies. *See also* CRIME; CUSTOMS; ICEBREAKER; MARITIME HAZARDS; MARITIME LAW; PIRACY; SHIPS AND BOATS, SAFETY OF.

Collector Cars

see Vintage Cars.

Communication Systems

Communication—transmitting information and ideas from one person to another—is closely linked to transportation. On the one hand, various types of communication systems play a critical role in directing or monitoring the movement of people and goods. On the other, ships, trains, motor vehicles, and planes actually carry messages—in the form of mail—from senders to recipients.

In ancient times people sent information by messengers or a system of signals. Later they wrote out messages and transmitted the document by personal courier or some form of postal network. Communications were revolutionized in the 1800s and 1900s by a series of inventions and new technologies, starting with the telegraph, telephone, and radio. Today people can transmit information instantaneously to any place in the world as well as into space, and the communication systems that have emerged have become essential tools for modern transportation.

Related Entries
For information on related topics, refer to the articles mentioned at the end of this entry.

The Telegraph.   The first major advance in rapid, long-distance communications was the invention of the telegraph, a method of sending information over a wire by means of electrical signals. American inventor Samuel F. B. Morse developed the first practical telegraph in 1837. By 1860 much of the United States was linked by telegraph lines, often strung beside railroad tracks. The telegraph became the basic communication system for railroads, used to check on the location of trains and the status of sections of track. Railroads still use automated telegraph systems.

The first **transcontinental** telegraph line was completed in 1861, and a **transatlantic** telegraph cable connected North America and Europe

transcontinental extending across a continent
transatlantic relating to crossing the Atlantic Ocean

Modern technology makes it possible to send information instantaneously to any place on the globe with electronic mail and cellular telephones.

five years later. By the early 1900s dozens of telegraph cables crossed the oceans, making it possible to send messages around the world.

The Telephone. In 1876 a Scottish-born Canadian inventor named Alexander Graham Bell developed the telephone, which could transmit a human voice over a wire. Telephone networks gradually spread throughout the world, linked by above- and below-ground telephone lines and undersea cables.

Technologies developed over the years have greatly improved the telephone. Thin cables containing optical fibers—fine strands of flexible glass—can carry thousands of phone calls at a time. One of the newest technologies is the cellular telephone, a device that uses radio transmitters and receivers to send voice messages through the air.

The telephone, the most important communications tool in everyday life, plays a significant role in transportation. All railroad systems are connected by telephone networks, and telephone communications are used in trucking, shipping, and the airline industry. Many motorists have cellular telephones in their cars.

The Radio. In 1895 Italian inventor Guglielmo Marconi used a device he called the wireless telegraph to send electronic signals through space. His invention, which later became known as the radio, revolutionized communications and made possible the later development of radar, television, cellular telephones, satellites, and other modern communication systems.

The radio plays a central role in transportation. All ships employ radio technology to maintain contact with each other and with facilities on shore. Train engineers, taxi drivers, bus drivers, subway operators, truckers, and others also use radio communication systems. Cellular telephone technology can sometimes be used in place of radio communications, but so far it is more expensive and generally less reliable.

Radio has a crucial function in air transportation, where it is not possible to communicate through wires. Airport control towers maintain contact with airplanes through two-way radio systems, and pilots in flight talk to each other through radios. Radio transmissions from ground facilities are used to activate electronic navigation systems on board airplanes, helping pilots during landing. A special kind of radio system called loran enables navigators on planes, as well as ships, to determine their position on Earth.

Space programs also depend enormously on radio communication systems. Astronauts in space talk with ground controllers by means of radio transmissions, and radio technology allows scientists and engineers on the ground to control satellites in space.

Radar. Developed during World War II, radar is a form of radio transmission that can detect objects within a certain range. A radar system transmits short, intense bursts of radio waves. When these waves meet an object, they bounce back, producing a radio echo that appears as an image on a radar screen. Radar has become a vital tool in shipping, aviation, weather, and highway traffic control.

Radar systems on ships help prevent collisions by detecting other vessels, coastlines, and obstacles. These systems are especially useful in fog or in bad weather when visibility is poor. Seaports rely on radar to observe and help guide ships entering or leaving the harbor, and busy waterways employ radar systems to monitor and control ship traffic.

Radar has a particularly important function in aviation. In airport control centers, radar is used to track planes in the air and to guide the movement of planes and other vehicles on runways. A device on airplanes called a radio altimeter uses radar technology to measure the plane's distance from the ground.

meteorologist scientist who studies weather and weather forecasting

Meteorologists use radar to identify weather patterns, providing vital information for planes, ships, and other forms of transportation. On the nation's highways, police rely on radar systems to detect speeding vehicles and to monitor traffic. In space programs, radar systems track spacecraft and satellites. Sonar, a similar system, is used by ships to detect objects under water.

Television. Although it is one of the world's most popular forms of communication and entertainment, television has a rather limited role in transportation. Television cameras mounted on railroad platforms allow station managers to observe passengers while making announcements to direct their movements. Cameras at railroad crossings enable controllers at distant stations to view the movement of cars and pedestrians near railroad tracks. Television cameras are also used to monitor and control the flow of motor vehicle traffic on some roads and streets.

Satellites. Satellites are the latest tool in long-distance communication. Equipped with electronic receivers and transmitters, they act as relay stations, forwarding radio broadcasts, television programs, and telephone calls quickly and efficiently from one place to another. The Global Positioning System (GPS), which uses information from satellites to determine a person's location on Earth to within a few feet, is used by some ships and planes to plot their positions. Certain new automobiles even offer GPS-based electronic road maps.

Computers. Most communication systems today are linked to and controlled in some way by computers. Computers process vast amounts of information that help communication systems function properly. They have been used to automate and greatly increase the efficiency of telephone and other communication systems. Most navigation and other electronic systems on planes and ships are controlled by computers, and computers play a crucial role in satellite communications.

See also AIR TRAFFIC CONTROL; DELIVERY SERVICES; GLOBAL POSITIONING SYSTEM (GPS); INTELSAT; LORAN; NAVIGATION; POSTAL SERVICE; RADAR; SATELLITES; SIGNALING; SONAR.

Green Means Go?

Anyone who has driven on highways or walked across city streets is familiar with red-yellow-green traffic lights and knows what each color stands for. But traffic lights started out as railroad communication signals, and they originally had different meanings. A green light signified "proceed with caution" (today's yellow), and a clear light was used to indicate "go." However, when the colored lens of a signal light was broken, one railroad engineer—thinking he had the "go" sign—went through a closed switch and wrecked his train. By 1914 yellow had come to mean "caution," and green signified "go."

Commuter Trains

see Commuting; Urban Transportation.

Commuting

For much of human history, people generally worked near where they lived or just a short walk or horseback ride away. The idea of commuting—traveling a distance every workday from home to place of employment—did not take root until the development of the first urban transportation systems in the early 1800s.

Today commuting is a way of life for many people around the globe. In the United States approximately 100 million workers travel to work each day by car or truck. Another 6 million use some form of public transportation.

Early Commuting. Until modern times, most cities extended only a few miles in any direction and walking was the primary form of local transportation. Because commercial centers and residential areas were close to one another, people could easily go to their jobs on foot.

In the early 1800s the introduction of public transportation in large cities encouraged growth and expansion. Horse-drawn streetcars and omnibuses—buslike vehicles that could carry up to 50 passengers—went into service in urban areas, making it possible for people to travel farther from their homes to get to work. By 1853 New York City had 683 licensed omnibuses carrying 120,000 riders each day.

With the development of these and other early forms of mass transportation—ferries, railroads, cable cars, and electric streetcars—more and more workers began riding to their jobs. They also settled farther away from congested urban centers and commuted back to the cities to work.

Growth of Suburbs. Inexpensive public transportation made commuting possible for many people, opening the way for the development of suburbs. Previously, only wealthy people could afford to live in the country and travel regularly to the city by horse and carriage. As transportation systems grew and lowered their fares, middle-income workers were able to consider living outside the city.

One of the first suburbs in the United States was Brooklyn, New York. A ferry service linking Brooklyn to commercial centers on the

---

Further Information

To learn more about specific forms of transportation used for commuting, see the related articles listed at the end of this article.

In the United States, people use various forms of transportation to travel between home and work.

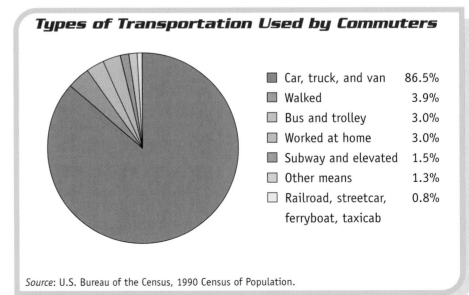

Types of Transportation Used by Commuters

■ Car, truck, and van	86.5%
■ Walked	3.9%
■ Bus and trolley	3.0%
■ Worked at home	3.0%
■ Subway and elevated	1.5%
■ Other means	1.3%
□ Railroad, streetcar, ferryboat, taxicab	0.8%

Source: U.S. Bureau of the Census, 1990 Census of Population.

island of Manhattan began operation in 1814 and expanded throughout the century.

By the late 1800s railroads and electric streetcars provided service to outlying areas of many cities. Most early suburbs developed within walking distance of streetcar lines. Railway stations, spaced some distance apart, gave rise to separate communities. As streetcar lines reached these areas—with frequent stops along the way—new neighborhoods filled in the gaps. Although the suburbs had their own political organizations, they remained closely tied socially and economically to the nearby cities.

By the early 1900s the movement to suburbs had increased significantly in many industrialized nations. The new communities attracted middle-class families seeking to escape urban dirt, noise, and congestion for country air and more spacious living arrangements. The commuters adjusted to a new rhythm—traveling from their suburban homes into the city's commercial district in the morning and reversing the journey at the day's end. They took railroads and streetcars to travel between their homes and the city, and **mass transit** systems to move about the urban area. Meanwhile, as families abandoned the city, businesses and factories moved in to their old neighborhoods. City dwellers who could not afford to relocate to the suburbs had to deal with the effects of this shift, the deterioration of the inner city.

mass transit *system of public transportation in an urban area*

Urban Transportation. Following on the success of the early omnibuses, a variety of mass transit systems appeared in cities. In 1832 omnibus operators in New York City began installing rails in the streets to provide a smoother roadbed for the vehicles and reduce the energy needed to pull them. This was the beginning of the streetcar. By the mid-1800s horse-drawn streetcars that ran on tracks had become common throughout many of the world's major cities. An electric streetcar system began operation in 1888 in Richmond, Virginia. By the early 1900s there were more than 20,000 miles of streetcar track in the nation. Streetcars and other light rail systems are still an important form of transportation in many cities, particularly in Europe. A number of urban centers in the United States are considering plans for new light rail systems.

Cable cars, subways, and ferries also serve urban commuters. Introduced in San Francisco in 1873, the cable car could travel up and down the city's steep hills. The world's first subway system opened in London in 1863. It proved to be less expensive than other forms of urban transportation—and faster, because it avoided the street-level traffic. Between 1950 and 2000, many large cities in the United States and Canada built subway systems, including Atlanta; San Francisco; Washington, D.C.; Montreal; and Toronto.

Ferries have played an important role in urban areas located next to bodies of water. Although bridges replaced ferry systems in a number of places, in recent years increasing traffic congestion on bridges has made ferries an attractive alternative for commuters crossing rivers or harbors. In New Jersey, new lines have been added to the ferry services that take commuters across the Hudson River from Jersey City to Manhattan. Boston, New Orleans, Seattle, and Toronto also have major ferry operations.

Telecommuting

In recent years a very different type of commuting has been gaining ground—telecommuting. Telecommuting does not involve travel, just an electronic link between home and workplace that allows employees working at home to keep in touch with a central office. Telecommuters rely on telephone and computer networks, including fax and e-mail, to send and receive information and to communicate with colleagues. This arrangement reduces the amount of time spent on commuting, allows workers to enjoy more time with their families, and curbs traffic congestion, fuel consumption, and air pollution. Telecommuting is becoming an alternative to traveling to and from the workplace.

Trains provide regional service between suburbs and cities in many areas of the United States. Here, commuters in Connecticut wait for a train to New York City.

Motor-driven buses were first developed in the 1920s. Though descended from horse-drawn omnibuses, the modern vehicles are faster and more comfortable and can cover greater distances. Local bus companies serve people traveling within a city or suburb, while intercity buses carry commuters over greater distances. In 1990 nearly 3.5 million individuals in the United States used buses to travel to and from work.

Trolley buses powered by electricity are gaining favor in some urban areas because they are much less polluting than buses with gasoline and diesel engines. Philadelphia, San Francisco, and Vancouver, Canada, have trolley-bus networks.

Regional Services.

Many commuters ride railway trains that link cities and suburban areas. Major urban areas such as New York, Paris, London, Moscow, and Tokyo have commuter railroads that connect to subways, buses, and other forms of mass transit. In the United States about 75 percent of all railroad passengers are commuters. Since the 1970s some regions of the world have developed high-speed rail services that reduce the travel time of commuters. In France and Japan, for example, trains capable of traveling up to 160 miles per hour (257 km per hour) carry people to work from distant locations.

Very few people fly to work on a daily basis, but some make a weekly commute by plane. People who live far from their place of employment often establish a secondary residence near work and fly home for the weekend. Individuals who divide their time between two or more distant workplaces also travel by airplane.

Many people make regular work-related trips by air. Commuter airlines or air taxi services offer connecting flights between local or regional airports and large airports near major cities. The planes generally carry fewer than 20 passengers.

The Automobile.

The automobile revolutionized both commuting and suburban life. No longer dependent on public transportation, workers who had cars could live almost anywhere within a reasonable distance from their place of employment. Suburbs had been developing since the late 1800s, but the automobile contributed to their rapid expansion.

In the United States suburban growth became especially dramatic after the 1950s. By the 1970s more Americans lived in suburbs than in central cities. Today large numbers of suburbanites still commute to the city. But over the years many businesses and industries have moved to the suburbs, and others have sprung up to provide goods and services for local residents. These businesses often employ people who commute to work within or between suburbs, a pattern known as lateral commuting. Some workers even travel in the opposite direction—from their homes in the city to work in the suburbs.

To accommodate the increase in automobile use, governments launched extensive highway construction programs. One of the first was completed in 1925 and covered the New York **metropolitan** area. The freeway system of Los Angeles—one of the world's most extensive highway networks—carries millions of commuters each day.

metropolitan relating to a large city and the surrounding surburbs

The expansion of commuter highway systems has spread suburban growth far into the countryside, creating small commuter communities known as exurbs. People living in exurbs may sometimes commute 50 miles (80 km) or more to work in cities or in intermediate suburban areas. At the same time, the long distance between home and workplace has led to a revival of commuter rail systems.

Commuting and Society. Commuting has created opportunities for individuals to live and work in separate locations. However, it has also put great strains on society, contributing to air pollution, lost business productivity, and increased levels of stress. Traveling to and from a job increases the length of the workday for many people and causes them to spend a great deal of time away from their families. Delays due to traffic take up additional time, and bad weather can make driving hazardous. During rush hour—the morning and evening periods when vast numbers of commuters are on the road—tie-ups can be even worse. The many motor vehicles used by commuters cause urban highway systems to deteriorate rapidly, requiring costly repairs. The increase in commuting also results in greater fuel consumption.

Highway authorities have established various programs to help the daily commute go more smoothly. For example, they have designated certain parts of roadways as high occupancy vehicle (HOV) lanes. Cars using them during peak hours must contain at least two—and, in some locations, three—people. Excluding all other cars and trucks from HOV lanes reduces congestion, enabling the traffic in these lanes to move faster. Transportation planners also look for ways to speed commuters through toll plazas. In New York, drivers can use the E-Z Pass system to whiz through toll booths. When an electronic device in the toll booth detects a sensor placed in the front of a car, it charges the toll payment directly to the driver's credit card account.

Many experts see public transportation as a solution to the traffic and pollution problems. Buses, trains, and light rail systems can handle large numbers of commuters more efficiently than automobiles and with less damage to the environment. Most European nations rely heavily on public transportation to meet commuter needs. In the United States, many metropolitan areas are trying to promote the use of public transportation by improving rail and subway systems, adding ferry service to help reduce bridge traffic, and encouraging people to carpool—to share the journey to and from work instead of driving alone. *See also* AMTRAK; AUTOMOBILES, EFFECTS OF; BART (BAY AREA RAPID TRANSIT); BUSES; CABLE CARS AND FUNICULARS; CONRAIL; FERRIES; GOVERNMENT AND TRANSPORTATION; LIGHT RAIL SYSTEMS; PUBLIC TRANSPORTATION; ROADS; TRANSPORTATION IN THE TWENTY-FIRST CENTURY; URBAN TRANSPORTATION.

Compass

The compass, a device used to determine direction, is an essential instrument in navigation. Installed on ships, aircraft, and some land vehicles, compasses are also carried by hikers who venture off the beaten path. Over the centuries, improvements and modifications have made compasses reliable in a wide variety of conditions.

Lodestones and Needles.

In ancient times navigators determined direction by observing the position of the Sun or the North Star. Then in the 1100s, mariners in China and the Mediterranean region discovered the directional properties of lodestone, a type of magnetic ore. When floated on a piece of wood in a bowl of water, a bar of lodestone points north. The bar's two magnetic poles—north and south—align with the Earth's own magnetic poles. With a lodestone compass, mariners could find direction even under cloudy skies.

Sailors also found that an iron needle placed near a lodestone eventually becomes magnetized. They stuck a magnetized needle through a piece of straw or cork and set it afloat in the compass bowl. For a more accurate reading, a vertical pin could be placed in the bottom of the bowl to support a card marked with the points of the compass, with the magnetic needle floating on top. Later compasses were encased in glass to make them more stable and accurate.

Variation and Deviation.

In the 1400s mariners realized that magnetic compasses do not point to the geographic North Pole. This happens because the Earth's magnetic field is not directly in line with its geographic north-south axis. The difference, or variation, between geographic north and magnetic north—the point indicated by the compass needle—depends on the observer's position on the Earth's surface. To deal with this problem, navigators compiled detailed charts showing the amount of variation at any location.

During the 1800s, when iron began to replace wood in ships, sailors noticed that the metal affected the position of the compass needle. Inventors compensated for this effect—called deviation—by placing magnets and unmagnetized iron pieces around the compass.

Gyrocompasses.

A new compass design appeared in the early 1900s. It incorporated a gyroscope—a disk that spins on an axis and resists changes in its direction. A magnetic compass mounted on a gyroscope is less affected by a shifting environment, such as the rolling of a ship at sea. However, these gyromagnetic compasses are still too unstable for use on aircraft. Modern planes and large ships use a gyrocompass, which contains a motor-driven gyroscope that provides a steady indication of direction. *See also* GYROSCOPE; NAVIGATION.

Concorde

supersonic faster than the speed of sound

prototype first working example of a new design

The Concorde is a **supersonic** transport plane (SST), capable of flying faster than the speed of sound. In 1962 the governments of Great Britain and France provided money to two companies—the British Aircraft Corporation and France's Aérospatiale—for the development of a high-speed passenger plane. The **prototype** of the Concorde flew on March 2, 1969, and production began soon afterward. British Airways and Air France put the plane into service in 1976.

The Concorde was neither the only SST nor the first SST to make a successful flight. That record was held by the Soviet Tupolev Tu-144, which flew in December 1968. But after a Tu-144 disintegrated in midair at the 1973 Paris Air Show, the Soviet Union put its plans for this plane on hold.

Flown by Air France and British Airways, the Concorde can cross the Atlantic Ocean in less than four hours.

Powered by four turbojet engines, the Concorde flies at a cruising speed of 1,350 miles per hour (2,170 km per hour). It can reach a top speed of over Mach 2 (twice the speed of sound) and maintain an altitude of up to about 11 miles (18 km). However, the Concorde has had two major problems—noise and cost. Its high noise level has led many countries to refuse it permission to enter their airspace. Tickets are extremely expensive because the plane has high operating costs and carries only 100 passengers. Although production was halted in 1979 after the construction of 16 planes, the Concorde continues to fly across the Atlantic. *See also* AIRCRAFT; ENGINES; JET PLANES; NOISE CONTROL; SUPERSONIC FLIGHT.

Conestoga Wagons

Made of wood and often painted blue and red, the Conestoga wagon was developed to meet the demands of the North American frontier. After 1750 it became the principal means of transporting goods between the Atlantic coast and the Ohio River valley. Swiss and German immigrants of the Conestoga Valley in eastern Pennsylvania had created the wagon in the early 1700s.

Several features of the Conestoga wagon made it particularly well suited for the rough, hilly roads of the rapidly growing region. The wagon's wide-rimmed wheels kept it from bogging down in mud. Its sturdy body curved up at both ends and had high panels all around so that goods would not slide out when the wagon went up and down hills or over bumps. Its cargo could be protected from wind, rain, and snow by attaching a canvas top to a set of wooden hoops

Throughout the 1700s and 1800s, many American settlers traveled westward in Conestoga wagons. This photo shows a Conestoga wagon along the Lincoln Highway just west of Philadelphia.

schooner *fast, easy-to-maneuver sailing ship with two or more masts and triangular sails*

over the wagon bed. Moreover, the wagon body could float across rivers like a boat once its wheels had been removed.

Pulled by four to six horses, Conestoga wagons could carry up to 6 tons of cargo. When American settlers began moving west of the Appalachian Mountains after the Revolutionary War, the Conestoga wagon proved to be the perfect vehicle for transporting goods to the frontier. In the early years of the 1800s, long lines of wagons traveled the country's growing network of roads, highways, and turnpikes. German settlers from Pennsylvania traveled to the Grand River valley in southern Ontario in Conestoga wagons.

The glory days of the Conestoga wagon ended in the mid-1800s, when railroads began crossing the Appalachian and Allegheny mountain ranges. But, at the same time, a new version of the wagon appeared farther west. Flatter and with lower sides than the Conestoga wagon, the prairie schooner was used by thousands of settlers heading for Oregon and California. This new wagon earned its name because its white canvas top resembled the sail of a **schooner** on the prairie horizon. *See also* CARTS, CARRIAGES, AND WAGONS; HORSES.

Conrail

Conrail (short for Consolidated Rail Corporation) was a major freight-carrying railroad in the northeastern and midwestern United States for more than 20 years. In 1973 the U.S. Congress passed the Regional Rail Reorganization Act, which created a new rail freight system to replace the failing Penn Central Transportation and five other bankrupt railroads. The government owned 85 percent of Conrail's stock. Conrail began operations on April 1, 1976, with an investment of $2.1 billion to modernize its tracks and equipment.

To cut costs, Conrail immediately sold some of its tracks to Amtrak and abandoned unprofitable routes. However, the company still required heavy government funding to stay in business, and it lost money for several years. In 1981 Conrail hired L. Stanley Crane as president to streamline the organization. Crane raised productivity, increased the marketing efforts of the company, drastically reduced the number of employees, and sold all the commuter rail lines to concentrate on carrying freight. That year Conrail showed a profit for the first time.

Although pleased by Conrail's success, the administration of President Ronald Reagan was opposed to government ownership of the railroad. A law passed in 1981 called for Conrail to be sold to private parties as soon as the company had reached a certain level of profitability. Six years later the government sold its Conrail stock, and the company continued to prosper as a private corporation. In 1998 two other railroad corporations—CSX and Norfolk Southern—acquired Conrail. The following year they divided most of the company's routes, incorporating them into their own railway networks. *See also* AMTRAK; FREIGHT TRAINS; GOVERNMENT AND TRANSPORTATION; RAILROAD INDUSTRY.

Containerization

Containerization is a method of transporting cargo by packing many items together in large boxlike containers. This process has revolutionized the freight industry, becoming a fundamental part of trucking and shipping. It also plays a major role in moving freight by rail and air.

Traditional Freight Transport. Before the development of containerization, workers had to transfer and pack small packages of cargo repeatedly between the point of manufacture and the point of delivery. This method required much time and labor, and it provided numerous opportunities for breakage, theft, and other loss of cargo. In addition, the loading and unloading of shipments was held up whenever dockers called a strike.

The practice of packing cargo in containers began in 1929 when a U.S. firm shipped full railroad boxcars to Cuba. During World War II, shippers used similar-sized crates in an attempt to streamline the process and speed the delivery of military supplies. This practice fell out of favor after the war, but it was revived in the 1960s and soon became the preferred method of shipping cargo.

Modern Containerization. The process of modern containerization begins at the factory. Goods are loaded into containers that are usually taken by truck from the factory to a rail yard or port for transfer onto railroad cars or ships. The container remains sealed until it arrives at its destination.

Most containers are about 8 feet (2.4 m) high, 8 feet (2.4 m) wide, and from 20 to 40 feet (6 to 12 m) long, although some cargo ships carry larger models and airplanes carry smaller ones. Many shipping companies use containers in standard sizes so that procedures and equipment for handling them can also be standardized. Generally made of steel, aluminum, or reinforced plywood, containers are strong and waterproof. Special versions include refrigerated containers, heated containers, and tank containers.

Shipbuilders have designed several vessels to carry containers. The most common is the containership, which can hold hundreds of standard-sized containers. The LASH (lighter aboard ship) vessel has its own crane for moving floating containers called lighters. A roll-on/roll-off vessel holds wheeled containers that load and unload through openings on the ends or sides of the ship.

Many seaports and railroad freight terminals have cranes and other equipment for handling containers. They often use computers to control the sequence of loading and unloading. In the past it took many days to load and unload large cargo ships, which spent about half of the time in port. Containerships can be processed in 36 hours or less. The fast turnaround allows shippers to increase the amount of cargo they carry in a given period or to reduce the size of their fleet. The same is true for rail companies. The increased efficiency of containerization has helped reduce the cost and time required for freight transportation. Today long trains of double-stacked containers are operated from coast to coast. *See also* CARGO SHIPS; FREIGHT; FREIGHT TRAINS; HARBORS AND PORTS; SHIPPING INDUSTRY; TRUCKING INDUSTRY.

Containerization greatly increases the efficiency of freight transportation. With the use of standard-size containers, shippers can load and unload their ships in less than two days.

Convertibles

Convertibles are automobiles with tops that may be folded back according to the weather and the owner's preference. Designed for pleasure rather than for practical transport, convertibles present an image of a glamorous, carefree lifestyle. The style is popular for luxury automobiles and sports cars.

The earliest autos were open to the wind and sky. Between 1905 and 1925, most had folding tops. However, as car sales increased, manufacturers added new features, such as a roof and windows, to make automobile travel more comfortable.

Although roofs became standard on cars, not every driver wished to sit in a small, enclosed space. Some sports cars of the 1920s and 1930s remained open. As a compromise, manufacturers developed convertible options for certain models. These cars had either a hard roof that could be removed and replaced or a soft, cloth roof that could fold back like the bellows of an accordion.

During the period of prosperity that followed World War II, sporty convertibles became very popular in the United States. They were often used for public appearances by politicians, movie stars, and other celebrities. However, critics raised concerns about safety. They pointed out that if a convertible flipped over in an accident, its driver and passengers could suffer serious injury or death. In response, manufacturers began to add a metal arc—known as a roll bar—above the seats. The roll bar holds its shape under the weight of a flipped car, protecting the passengers from contact with the road.

Despite this improvement, convertibles never recovered their former appeal. Safety remained a concern. Furthermore, many drivers want the heating, air-conditioning, and stereo systems available in hard-topped cars and prefer the enclosed environment—which shuts out much of the highway's noise and exhaust fumes—to open-air driving. *See also* SPORTS CARS; VINTAGE CARS.

Conveyors

Conveyors are mechanical devices that convey, or move, materials along a fixed path. Businesses and industries have found numerous uses for conveyors, especially when transporting large amounts of goods at a continuous rate.

Some conveyors use gravity or physical labor to move things; others are driven by motors. Conveyors can carry objects in a straight line or around curves, across a flat plane, or up and down an **incline.** The kind of conveyor selected depends on the material to be transported. Complicated tasks may require a series of different conveyors.

incline *surface that slants*

Nonpowered Conveyors.
Chutes and roller and wheel conveyors operate without mechanical or electrical power. Chutes are channels through which materials flow, sliding down by the force of gravity. They are usually set on an incline between different levels and may follow straight or curved paths. People use chutes to move bulky materials such as coal and gravel, but only in a downward direction.

Roller conveyors consist of a series of cylindrical rods set into a frame. Wheel conveyors have wheels instead of rollers, mounted on axles in the frame. When such conveyors are placed on an incline, gravity draws objects down, and friction limits their speed. Along a flat run, objects must be pushed or pulled by hand. Because they lack power, roller and wheel conveyors are generally used only over short distances for moving boxes or other objects with smooth, firm surfaces. They can be especially useful for loading and unloading packages from transport vehicles.

Power-Driven Conveyors. Most conveyors have power supplied by a motor, and they move material by means of a belt, chain, or cable. A belt conveyor consists of a flat, continuous loop of rubber, plastic, metal, fabric, or leather, often supported by a series of rollers. The belt loops around a pulley at each end; one of the pulleys—the drive pulley—is connected to the motor. These conveyors can run in a flat line or on an incline, depending on the material to be moved. Some have raised sides to form a trough or partitions to create compartments, making it possible to transport loose substances such as grain. Belt conveyors can also carry people, as do the moving sidewalks used by passengers in airports.

Conveyors that are equipped with chains or cables operate on the same principle as belt conveyors. A motor drives the loop of chain or cable, which moves along a system of wheels and gears. Buckets, baskets, or hooks may be attached to the chain or cable to carry the material. Chain and cable conveyors usually have greater flexibility than belt conveyors. They can follow curved paths easily and be used on steep inclines. The famous cable cars of San Francisco are pulled by a cable conveyor system below the street. Auto manufacturing plants often use overhead chain conveyors to carry heavy parts along an **assembly line.**

assembly line *production system in which tasks are performed in sequence by an arrangement of workers and equipment*

The screw conveyor, another common type, has a twisted shaft that rotates in place and pushes things along its length. Other types of conveyors use vibrations and air suction to move materials through tubes. *See also* Cable Cars and Funiculars; People Movers.

Convoys

A convoy is a group of merchant ships sailing together for protection, usually with a warship escort. Convoys have been used since ancient times to protect ships against pirates, but early trading vessels were generally armed and defended each other rather than relying on a warship. In the 1200s England began to use armed escort vessels to protect its merchant ships and troop transports from attack. The English system served as the model for modern convoys. In colonial times, Spanish galleons loaded with cargo were accompanied by heavily armed escort ships on their trips across the Atlantic. During World War I and World War II, Britain and the United States used convoys to shield merchant ships against German submarine and surface attacks. World War II convoys relied on air cover as well as naval protection to help defend commercial shipping. *See also* Merchant Marine.

Cook, Thomas
British travel pioneer

Thomas Cook started the first travel agency during the mid-1800s in England. Over time his services included rail tours of Europe, sightseeing cruises along rivers, and guided tours overseas.

Thomas Cook, a British missionary, invented the modern industries of tourism and travel. In the mid-1800s he led the first organized tours and established the first travel agency.

Born in Melbourne, England, in 1808, Cook left school at the age of 10 and became a Baptist missionary at age 20. He strongly supported the temperance movement, which encouraged people not to drink alcohol. Cook's enthusiasm for temperance led him into a new profession. In 1841 he persuaded a railway company to arrange a special train for 570 people traveling to a temperance meeting in a town 20 miles (32 km) distant. Travel historians regard that trip as the first advertised tour in history. It included transportation, meals, musical entertainment, and Cook's service as a guide.

Cook went on to organize other temperance tours and then began arranging excursions for all kinds of travelers. The railways paid him a small commission for each traveler he signed up for a rail ticket. In 1855 he conducted his first tour outside England, leading excursions across the English Channel to France.

The following year Cook arranged a "Grand Tour of Europe," personally guiding English tourists through Belgium, Germany, and France for a reasonable price. Wealthy and aristocratic young men had been making such trips for a long time, but Cook brought tourism within the reach of the middle class and launched a revolution in travel.

During the 1860s Cook focused on expanding his business, which sold travel tickets and organized tour packages. A shrewd businessman, he received discounts from railway companies and hotels, which were eager to welcome his large groups of customers. His son, John Mason Cook, joined him in the business and set up an office in the United States. Thomas Cook and Son, the first travel agency, dominated the young industry for many years. Cook died in 1892, but his firm remains in business today with many offices worldwide.

Cook's tours tended to move quickly, spending just a short time at each of their many stops. Some criticized this approach, but his trips opened the world to many who otherwise would never have traveled. Morever, they created the modern travel and tour industries, which spurred the growth of railroads, shipping lines, and other forms of passenger transportation. *See also* Tourism; Travel Industry.

Cosmonauts

Soviet Union *nation that existed from 1922 to 1991, made up of Russia and 14 other republics in eastern Europe and northern Asia*

Cosmonauts are individuals in the Russian space program who travel into space. The name comes from the Greek words meaning "sailor of the universe." The responsibilities of cosmonauts include such functions as piloting spacecraft, operating space stations, repairing satellites, and conducting scientific experiments in space—much the same as the work performed by American astronauts. In the early years of space travel, cosmonauts and astronauts worked separately because of the fierce rivalry between the **Soviet Union** and the United States. Since the collapse of the Soviet Union in 1991, however, cosmonauts and astronauts have cooperated on several multinational missions.

Achievements in Space. In 1957 the Soviet Union launched *Sputnik,* the world's first satellite, into space. In the following years it remained ahead of the United States in space research and technology, and Soviet cosmonauts achieved many important goals. On April 12, 1961, Yuri Gagarin became the first person in space, orbiting the Earth once in a space capsule. Two years later the Soviets sent the first woman into space, Valentina Tereshkova. On March 18, 1965, Alexei Leonov made the first walk outside a craft orbiting in space. However, rocket development problems prevented Soviet cosmonauts from planning a mission to land on the Moon.

Cosmonauts established the first space station, *Salyut 1,* in June 1971. Crew members Georgy Dobrovolsky, Viktor Patsayev, and Vladislav Volkov spent 24 days aboard the station, conducting various scientific and medical studies. All three died tragically during their return to Earth, when the cabin of their spacecraft, *Soyuz 11,* suddenly lost air pressure.

Despite this disaster, Soviet cosmonauts continued to work in Salyut space stations and later aboard the space station *Mir,* which flew for more than 12 years in the 1980s and 1990s. They have set numerous endurance records for time spent in orbit and have contributed greatly to knowledge about the effects of life in space on the human body.

Background and Training of Cosmonauts.

The first cosmonauts were experienced military pilots, chosen for their skill, courage, and ability to withstand demanding physical conditions. As the roles of cosmonauts expanded, people with backgrounds in engineering, science, and medicine also entered the developing space program. Participants in the Soviet and Russian space program have also included men and women from Bulgaria, Cuba, France, Germany, Hungary, India, Mongolia, Poland, Romania, Syria, and Vietnam.

Most cosmonaut training takes place at the Gagarin Center near Moscow. Also known as Star City, the center houses the trainees and many different laboratories and facilities. All cosmonaut candidates undergo rigorous testing to determine their physical, mental, and emotional fitness for spaceflight and their ability to handle any emergencies that may arise. Those who pass receive more training to develop these skills, including physical exercise and lessons in parachuting and wilderness survival. To prepare for the special conditions of spaceflight, cosmonauts also experience simulations of acceleration and weightlessness.

aerodynamics branch of science that deals with the motion of air and the effects of such motion on planes and other objects

Scientific training is equally thorough and demanding. Cosmonauts study astronomy, computers, navigation, **aerodynamics,** and other sciences. They learn about rockets, space stations, and other spacecraft, and they must master the complex mechanical and electronic systems that operate these vehicles. Training may take as long as eight to ten years in all.

After completing the basic program, cosmonauts continue to train while waiting to be assigned to a mission. Each mission also requires specific instruction from scientists and engineers who teach the cosmonauts to conduct particular experiments and procedures.

In the 1990s political and economic difficulties in Russia seriously limited the country's space program. As a result, cosmonauts had fewer opportunities to travel into space. Even so, Russia has continued to cooperate with other nations in space, and it is participating in the construction of a new international space station. *See also* ASTRONAUTS; GAGARIN, YURI; LEONOV, ALEXEI; MIR; SALYUT SPACE STATIONS; SOYUZ SPACECRAFT; SPACE EXPLORATION; SPACE STATIONS; SPACE TRAVEL; SPACE VEHICLES; SPACE WALKS; TERESHKOVA, VALENTINA.

Crime

Crime related to transportation is as old as travel itself. Since ancient times, the movement of people and goods has offered opportunities for gain—both legal and illegal. Indeed, transporting goods always involves an element of risk along with the chance to earn a profit.

maritime related to the sea or shipping

Piracy. For as long as people have been engaged in **maritime** trade, seafaring robbers known as pirates, buccaneers, corsairs, sea rovers, and freebooters have sailed the globe in search of treasure. The illegal seizure of property on the high seas is known as piracy.

Pirates plagued the commerce of seafaring peoples of the ancient world in the Mediterranean region. The Romans cleared the area of pirates, making the Mediterranean safe for shipping for many years. But as Roman power faded, piracy returned with force.

tribute payment made to a dominant power

During the Middle Ages, Viking raiders terrorized ships and settlements along the coasts of northern Europe. In the Mediterranean, Barbary corsairs—Muslim pirates of North Africa—attacked ships from Christian states, selling captives into slavery and demanding **tribute** for protection against attack. Piracy in the Mediterranean had such a disastrous effect on shipping that Europeans sought other routes for trade—a major reason for the voyages of exploration that led to the European discovery of the Americas.

Piracy existed in other parts of the world as well. Throughout much of Asia, a variety of marauders terrorized sea routes and coastal areas from earliest times. Asian piracy expanded greatly in the 1600s as European trade to the region increased. In the Americas, piracy flourished in the Caribbean Sea during the 1500s and 1600s. Many Caribbean buccaneers began their careers as **privateers** in the service of a nation. When their official employment ended, they continued to plunder ships on their own.

privateer privately owned ship authorized by a government to attack enemy vessels; also, the individual who commands the ship

Piracy remained a threat to shipping until the 1800s, when naval warships of Great Britain and other nations cleared the seas of most pirates and began protecting merchant vessels. Today it survives in Southeast Asia, where modern-day pirates armed with speedboats and automatic weapons prey on fishing boats and small merchant vessels.

customs tax on imported goods

Smuggling. People have engaged in smuggling—the illegal movement of goods across national borders—since governments first began to regulate trade and to tax imported goods. Smuggling developed as a way to avoid paying **customs** and to get around trade restrictions.

Smuggling has flourished in many eras. In the 1700s Britain's strict policies on shipping and trade with its American colonies resulted in a substantial amount of illegal commerce. In the 1920s and 1930s, laws banning the sale of liquor in the United States led to widespread smuggling, with ships carrying illegal liquor to small ports along the

Atlantic coast and trucks and automobiles smuggling it across the Canadian border.

Smuggling continues in modern times. Among the items most commonly trafficked are illegal drugs, weapons, gemstones, exotic animals, and illegal immigrants. Modern smugglers devise many ingenious ways to hide **contraband** and transport it by means of airplane, train, ship, truck, and automobile.

contraband items imported or exported illegally

Robbery and Theft.

Throughout history the road has been a dangerous place, especially in remote areas. Travelers tried to protect themselves from robbers. In the 1200s the king of England took steps to reduce the incidence of highway robbery by ordering brush to be cleared from the sides of roads, thus removing possible hiding places for "highwaymen."

During the westward expansion of the United States, stagecoach and train robberies occurred with disturbing frequency. In the 1920s and 1930s bank robbers such as John Dillinger and Baby Face Nelson used automobiles to get away quickly after a holdup. Today traveling by car or train is generally quite safe. Highway robbery is most likely to take place in remote areas of developing countries where there is little law enforcement. However, automobile theft is a common problem in the United States and many other countries. The stolen vehicles are often disassembled and their parts sold.

Hijacking.

Hijacking is the unlawful seizure of an airplane, ship, or other vehicle. The hijacking of airplanes, also known as skyjacking, became a growing problem in the 1960s and 1970s. Many skyjackers had political motives. Terrorist groups, in particular, hijacked planes as a way to punish enemies or draw attention to their cause. The number of skyjackings has decreased dramatically since the 1980s as a result of improved airport security.

Ships, trucks, and cars have also been the target of hijackings. Ships have occasionally been hijacked, but it is difficult to take control of them. However, in 1985 a group of terrorists seized the Italian cruise ship *Achille Lauro*. One American passenger was killed during the takeover. From time to time, trucks are hijacked for their cargoes. Carjacking, the theft of an automobile by force, has become a growing problem in recent years. But it is far less common than ordinary car theft.

Preventing Transportation-Related Crime.

Before the creation of police forces and border guards, travelers often made arrangements to protect themselves from crime along their routes. Early traders and merchants hired bodyguards to defend them from bandits and thieves. For thousands of years, merchant ships carried weapons or armed their crews to fight pirates.

Official protection of travelers has typically been provided by law enforcement groups organized by the government. By the mid-1800s, national navies had become strong enough to protect merchant ships on a regular basis. Similarly, the development of police forces helped make traveling on roads safer.

Your Money or Your Life, Please

The highwaymen who preyed on English travelers in the 1600s and 1700s were a diverse group. Although there were plenty of thugs and ruffians among them, their numbers also included noblemen who had lost their fortunes and even the sons of clergymen. Often these "gentleman" robbers demanded money with great courtesy—though they were not above killing if crossed. Foreign visitors to England complained about the many thieves on English highways but remarked on their often charming manners.

Modern nations employ various agencies to fight travel-related crime. Navies and coast guards watch over shipping and work with customs officials to combat smuggling. The state and local police who patrol roads and highways have responsibility for protecting travelers and those transporting goods. In the United States, the Federal Aviation Administration (FAA) works with airlines and airports to guard against hijacking, and the Federal Bureau of Investigation (FBI) investigates such crimes. An international organization, Interpol, gathers and distributes information to law enforcement agencies around the world on criminal activities including smuggling and hijacking. Advances in the communications and **surveillance** technology used by such groups will help protect travelers and cargoes around the globe. *See also* COAST GUARD; CUSTOMS; HIJACKING; PIRACY; SMUGGLING.

surveillance close observation of a person, group, or activity

Cruise Ships

Cruise ships are vessels that offer passengers a voyage at sea in a comfortable setting with entertainment and sightseeing. Developed by shipping companies in the 1920s, cruises now form a significant part of the tourism industry.

The Emergence of the Cruise Ship.
Ocean liners of the early 1900s set the stage for the development of cruise ships. By the 1920s many liners—particularly those traveling between the United States and Europe—provided comfortable and often luxurious accommodations for their passengers. Shipping lines competed to provide the fastest and most elegant service along particular routes. Because travel declined during the winter months, some companies began using their liners to take vacationers on cruises at this time of year, sailing in the Mediterranean Sea or in other warm regions of the world.

In the late 1950s, when passenger airline service became widely available, the regular routes of ocean liners suffered. Many travelers chose to fly rather than make a long sea voyage. Unable to compete with the airlines, shipping companies abandoned many of their former routes and focused on offering pleasure cruises in areas of special interest to tourists. Instead of being a means of getting to a destination, the cruise ship became a destination in itself, a seagoing hotel with fine food, entertainment, visits to interesting ports, and a variety of onboard activities.

The Modern Cruise Industry.
By the late 1990s the cruise industry was serving more than 5 million passengers a year. Dozens of companies operated cruise ships, with some preparing to add new vessels to their fleets.

Ships range from small luxury yachts that carry no more than a dozen passengers to the 2,600-passenger *Grand Princess*. In general, the trend is toward larger ships, many weighing over 100,000 tons. Most have multiple decks, with dining rooms, activity areas, and swimming pools located on the upper decks and passenger cabins on the lower decks. Ships designed for travel in warm climates have open deck space for outdoor activities.

Modern cruise ships travel to popular locations such as Alaska and the Caribbean and Mediterranean Seas. In this photo, a luxury liner docks on the Nile River in Egypt.

Cruises range in length from a weekend break among closely spaced islands in the Bahamas to a round-the-world journey lasting months. The level of luxury also varies. Many cruises offer food and accommodations similar to those available in standard hotels, with more comfortable rooms available at a higher price. A small number of top-of-the-line cruises specialize in superior service, with sumptuous cuisine and surroundings to match.

Popular locations include the Caribbean Sea, Mexico, Alaska, Hawaii, New England, the Mediterranean Sea, and northern Europe. Although warm-water routes account for the majority of cruises taken by North Americans, cruise ships also visit colder regions, such as Antarctica.

Some companies offer specialty cruises—voyages organized around particular interests—such as scuba diving, jazz music, whale watching, or photography. They include activities and often stops related to the theme of the trip. For passengers with ample time and money, the ultimate ocean voyage is the world cruise, which visits numerous exotic ports as it circles the globe. *See also* OCEAN LINERS; SHIPS AND BOATS, TYPES OF; TOURISM.

Crusades

Between the late 1000s and 1300, a series of religious expeditions known as the Crusades left Europe for the Holy Land of Palestine in the Middle East. Those who took part—hundreds of thousands of Christian nobles, knights, peasants, townspeople, and even children—were on a mission to recapture the birthplace of Christianity from the Muslims.

For over 400 years Muslim Arabs had allowed European pilgrims to visit the Holy Land, and the Arabs played an important role in commerce between Europe and Asia. But the situation changed in the 1000s when the Seljuk Turks—Muslims from central Asia—invaded and conquered Palestine. In addition to preventing Christians from visiting the

The age of the Crusades lasted from the late 1000s to 1300. During this period Christians traveled from all parts of Europe in an attempt to regain the Holy Land from the Muslims. Although the expeditions did not accomplish this goal, they did stimulate the exchange of goods and knowledge between Europe and the East.

Holy Land, the Turks interfered with trade and threatened the security of the Byzantine Empire, a Christian kingdom centered in present-day Greece and Turkey.

In 1095 Pope Urban II, the head of the Christian Church in Rome, responded to the Muslim advance by calling for a Christian army to launch an expedition to the Middle East. After capturing part of the Holy Land, the leaders of this First Crusade divided the conquered territory into Christian states.

The Christian victory proved to be only temporary. When the Muslims continued to expand their influence, additional crusades were launched against them. Eight major crusades took place between 1095 and 1270, including one led by the German emperor Frederick Barbarossa, King Richard the Lion-Hearted of England, and King Philip II of France. Some of the expeditions ended in tragedy, particularly the Children's Crusade of 1212 in which many young people from Europe lost their lives. By 1291 the Muslims had recaptured all of the Holy Land.

The Crusades had a number of important effects on Europe. They increased contact with the Muslim cultures of the Middle East, introducing new ideas into European life. They stimulated the economic growth of cities, such as Italian ports on the Mediterranean Sea, that provided the armies with supplies. The movement of hundreds of thousands of people between Europe and the Middle East also opened new transportation routes between the two regions.

Cumberland Road

see National Road.

Cunard Line

The Cunard Line began as a steamship company that carried passengers and mail across the Atlantic Ocean. The company built and operated some of the best-known modern passenger ships.

The line was the brainchild of Sir Samuel Cunard (1787–1865), a merchant from Halifax, Nova Scotia. After winning a contract from the British government to carry mail between England, Canada, and the United States, Cunard and his business partners formed the Cunard Line. It launched its first ship, the wooden *Britannia,* in 1840 and introduced iron steamships in the 1850s. Cunard ships were always considered the leaders in passenger transportation. In 1934 the Cunard Line absorbed its rival, the White Star Line.

During the 1900s Cunard launched a number of famous ships, including the *Mauretania* and *Lusitania* in 1907, the *Queen Mary* in 1936, and the *Queen Elizabeth* in 1938. Regarded by some **maritime** historians as the finest of all passenger liners, the *Queen Mary* and the *Queen Elizabeth* spent the early 1940s transporting Allied troops in World War II.

After the war, ocean liners flourished—until the 1950s, when **transatlantic** passengers began traveling by air instead of by sea. The Cunard Queens were taken out of service in the late 1960s, and the *Queen Mary* became a dockside museum in Long Beach, California.

maritime *related to the sea or shipping*

transatlantic *relating to crossing the Atlantic Ocean*

The company still operates several smaller ships, including the *Queen Elizabeth II,* that carry passengers on Atlantic crossings as well as cruises. *See also* CRUISE SHIPS; OCEAN LINERS; SHIPBUILDING; SHIPPING INDUSTRY; STEAMSHIP LINES.

Curtiss, Glenn
U.S. aviation pioneer

dirigible large aircraft filled with a lighter-than-air gas that keeps it aloft; similar to a blimp but with a rigid frame

Glenn Curtiss, an American aviator and aircraft designer, made important contributions to the development of the modern aircraft. Born in 1878, Curtiss began to work in aviation in 1904, when he designed and built an engine for the first successful **dirigible** to fly in the United States. In 1908 he became the first American to fly over a measured distance of 1 km (0.6 mile). He accomplished this feat in the *June Bug,* a plane he had helped design.

One of Curtiss's greatest contributions was the invention of the aileron, a movable surface on the wing that controls an airplane's movement from side to side. However, his invention led to a legal battle with the Wright brothers, who won the rights to the patent. After demonstrating that aircraft could land on and take off from ships, Curtiss built the first planes for the U.S. Navy. In 1911 he designed and developed the earliest successful amphibian, an aircraft that used floats for landing on water. The following year he built the first flying boat with a body capable of floating. During World War I, Curtiss's company produced over 5,000 aircraft, including the JN-4 trainers nicknamed "Jennies." Curtiss died in 1930. *See also* AIRCRAFT, PARTS OF; AVIATION, HISTORY OF; SEAPLANES; WRIGHT, ORVILLE AND WILBUR.

Customs

domestic relating to activities or products made within a country

tariff system of taxes on imported or exported goods

Every nation has its own laws regarding the goods that may be imported, the quantities allowed, and the products on which customs duties—or taxes—must be paid. These regulations apply to merchandise brought into a country by businesses as well as items carried by individuals. Customs duties provide a source of income for the government. They also protect **domestic** industries and agriculture by regulating the importation of foreign goods. In addition, various international treaties control the movement of certain substances, such as ivory and narcotics, across national borders.

U.S. Customs Service. Congress approved the collection of customs duties in 1789, mainly as a source of income for the young nation. With the Tariff Act of 1816, the focus of customs shifted to protecting American industries. During the next century customs agents in different parts of the country often followed their own rules, leading to complaints about the lack of uniformity in **tariffs.** In 1927 the Department of the Treasury created the Bureau of Customs to standardize customs enforcement throughout the United States.

The U.S. Customs Service has other important functions besides collecting duties. It plays a prominent role in preventing the smuggling of drugs, weapons, and other illegal items and in enforcing the regulations of various government departments. For instance, it works with the Department of Commerce in gathering statistical data and in controlling the

The job of the U.S. Customs Service is to enforce government regulations on importing and exporting goods. This photo shows a customs official searching the trunk of an automobile for illegal tobacco and alcohol.

Fruit Flies and Beagle Brigades

Many people consider customs to be a nuisance, but even a small piece of imported fruit can be dangerous. In 1980 the Mediterranean fruit fly entered the United States, possibly through a single orange. Although only a few of the tiny flies slipped through customs, they caused an agricultural crisis in California that caused millions of dollars worth of damage. To avoid such problems, the U.S. Department of Agriculture uses "beagle brigades"—dogs with highly sensitive noses that search luggage for hidden fruit or meat.

artifact ornament, tool, weapon, or other object made by humans

export of certain restricted products. It also assists the Department of Agriculture in blocking the entry of diseased fruits and vegetables.

Customs Procedures. An individual who enters the United States from a foreign country must fill out a customs declaration form stating the type and value of goods purchased abroad. A customs officer examines the form to determine whether the traveler must pay a duty and, if so, how much. Customs agents may also inspect the contents of passengers' baggage to identify taxable items.

Each U.S. resident is allowed to enter the country with up to $400 worth of foreign goods without paying duties. Anyone returning directly from a U.S. possession—American Samoa, Guam, or the U.S. Virgin Islands—may bring up to $1,200 worth of goods duty-free.

Any items over the specified amount are subject to a duty. A person who fails to declare taxable items may be charged with a federal crime and, if convicted, face a fine or even a prison sentence.

Forbidden and Restricted Items. Some imported items are subject to restrictions. Adults may bring into the United States duty-free up to 100 cigars and 200 cigarettes and up to 1 liter (1 quart) of alcohol. Several states, however, have laws prohibiting the importation of any alcohol or tobacco.

Certain items—including illegal drugs, obscene literature, lottery tickets, fireworks, dangerous toys, and switchblade knives—cannot be brought into the country at all. Firearms and ammunition may enter only with a permit from the Bureau of Alcohol, Tobacco, and Firearms. In most cases, importing automobiles manufactured overseas is not allowed unless the vehicles are modified to meet U.S. standards for safety and pollution controls.

In addition, U.S. law prohibits the importation of items classified as historical **artifacts,** or the cultural property of a foreign nation. Ancient coins, masks, sculptures, or other artworks that a country wants to keep within its borders may fall within this category of forbidden goods.

Finally, because of the danger of introducing disease or insects, travelers are not permitted to bring most kinds of meat, fruits, vegetables, and plants into the United States. Pets such as dogs and cats are allowed if the owner can prove that the animals are free of disease. But birds, fish, and other wildlife must be held and examined at the owner's expense until a veterinarian has confirmed that they are healthy. The government also works to protect endangered species by prohibiting the importation of these animals or items made from them. *See also* GOVERNMENT AND TRANSPORTATION; HEALTH ISSUES; PASSPORTS AND VISAS; SMUGGLING; TARIFFS.

Daimler, Gottlieb
German automotive pioneer

internal combustion engine *engine powered by burning a mixture of fuel and air inside narrow chambers called cylinders*

carburetor *device that supplies an explosive mixture of fuel and air to an engine*

Working with Wilhelm Maybach, Gottlieb Daimler developed the first successful high-speed **internal combustion engine.** Daimler's use of the engine to propel various types of carriages paved the way for the modern automobile.

Born in 1834, Daimler studied engineering in Stuttgart, Germany, and worked at several engineering companies. In 1872 he joined the firm of Nikolaus Otto, the inventor of the four-stroke internal combustion engine. Daimler began to investigate ways of improving Otto's engine. He became convinced that a lightweight, faster version would provide a good source of power for a vehicle. In 1882 Daimler and Maybach, another engineer at the firm, left to open a workshop of their own.

In 1885 the two men developed a **carburetor** that allowed them to use gasoline for fuel instead of the coal gas burned in Otto's engine. That same year they patented their own high-speed engine and mounted it on a bicycle equipped with two small side wheels. Over the next few years they installed engines in a horse-drawn carriage and a boat.

In 1889 they produced the first vehicle specifically designed as an automobile rather than just a carriage with an engine attached to it. Recognizing the car's commercial value, Daimler founded an automobile manufacturing company, Daimler-Motoren-Gesellschaft, to produce it. Shortly after Daimler's death in 1900, the company introduced the Mercedes—a line of cars named after the daughter of a Daimler dealer. *See also* AUTOMOBILES, HISTORY OF; AUTOMOBILES, PARTS OF; BENZ, CARL; ENGINES.

Delivery Services

Since ancient times, delivery services have existed to carry mail and other items from place to place. Today the business of transportation moves large quantities of goods in the form of freight or cargo but also handles small items such as individual letters and parcels. Even in the computer age, when people can send electronic communications from their homes and offices, documents and objects still need to change hands.

Modern delivery services range from bicycle messengers who zip across town with a satchel full of envelopes to computer-linked global networks involving thousands of workers and almost every means of transportation. Governments provide delivery services through official postal systems, and private companies offer similar services.

Early Mail Systems.

The ancient Egyptian, Chinese, Assyrian, and Persian empires all had postal networks. The rulers of these empires needed to communicate with their officials and military leaders over long distances. They developed systems that consisted of relay runners or riders, each responsible for a certain stretch of road.

The relay couriers passed messages from hand to hand. Because each of the couriers had to cover only a short distance, they could move quickly. Mail posted in this way could travel as far as 100 miles (161 km) in one day. The ancient Greek historian Herodotus described Persian message carriers with words that became the motto of the modern U.S. Postal Service: "Neither snow nor rain nor heat nor gloom of night stays these couriers from the swift completion of their appointed rounds."

The early postal systems existed for official use only. By the A.D. 200s, however, the Roman postal network had begun carrying some private mail as well. The Romans had the most highly developed delivery system of the ancient world, with paved roads and way stations called posthouses that served couriers and their horses.

The Aztecs of Mexico and the Inca of South America also developed relay systems to carry messages and parcels over long distances. Kublai Khan, the Mongol ruler of central Asia in the 1200s, oversaw a postal system with more than 10,000 stations.

Delivery Services for the Public.

During the 1400s, as trade and literacy expanded in Europe, increasing numbers of people had written messages to exchange. Merchants, **guilds,** universities, and religious organizations already operated their own mail services. New services appeared to deliver mail for anyone who could pay the fee. One of the first and largest private mail systems, operated by the Taxis family of Vienna, had more than 20,000 couriers across central Europe. Still, mail service remained slow, expensive, and unreliable.

By the early 1500s, both France and England had established government-sponsored postal systems. Though intended for official messages, these services were also used by the general population. Eventually, public postal systems emerged in Europe, and some private delivery services continued to operate as well.

The British Parliament granted Thomas Neale the right to organize a postal service in the American colonies in 1691. The British government took the service over in 1707 and ran it until the American Revolution. Britain's own post introduced several new features in the 1800s, such as using stamps to indicate prepaid postage fees. It also began delivering mail within Britain at a single rate, no matter how great the distance.

The Rise of Private Services.

The U.S. Postal Service is the only delivery service allowed to handle first-class mail with U.S. postage. It carries larger items through its Parcel Post service. But mail and packages can also be sent by various alternate services offered by private companies.

guild *organization of skilled workers in a craft or trade*

Delivery services use bicycles, mopeds, trains, trucks, and airplanes to carry goods quickly to their destinations.

The United Parcel Service (UPS) began in Seattle, Washington, in 1907 as a group of teenagers carrying parcels around town. UPS's early growth came from delivering department-store purchases to customers, and it has since developed into an international shipping firm that delivers more than 12 million packages and documents a day around the world.

Another well-known delivery firm, Federal Express, was formed in 1973. This company pioneered the overnight delivery business, using late-night airplane flights and employees—often college students—who would work into the early morning sorting packages. Federal Express serves about 200 countries with its own fleet of over 600 aircraft, handling more than 3 million parcels every day. Other delivery companies include Roadway Express, which offers service by truck throughout North America, and the Amtrak Express, which ships packages by train.

These and other private delivery companies provide a range of services for varying fees, with the fastest and farthest deliveries costing the most. They now transport a large portion of mail and parcels in the United States and around the world, presenting serious competition for public postal services. On the local level, home delivery by grocery stores, bakeries, and dairies—once quite common—exists only on a limited scale today. Most customers drive to supermarkets to do their own shopping.

Laws Governing Delivery Services. Companies that offer delivery services operate within a complicated web of laws, some of which have developed over centuries. The transport of goods in exchange for a fee is called carriage, and each nation has its own regulations. In addition, special sets of rules may apply to each form of transportation, such as shipping, railroads, highways, and aircraft.

In the United States, the main government agencies that oversee carriage are the Department of Transportation for railroads, highways, and air traffic and the Federal Maritime Commission for shipping.

Under the law, carriers such as delivery services are responsible for certain kinds of damage to or loss of the goods in their care. Many services offer customers optional insurance on their parcels. Carriers may also restrict the kinds of goods they will handle—most delivery services, for example, will not carry cash or explosives. *See also* CIVIL AERONAUTICS BOARD; FREIGHT; INTERSTATE COMMERCE COMMISSION; POSTAL SERVICE; TRANSPORTATION, U.S. DEPARTMENT OF.

Winged Messengers

Carrier pigeons are one of the oldest ways of sending messages over long distances. Certain breeds of the European rock pigeon, known as homing pigeons, have the ability to find their way home from a distant location. As early as 1150, the sultan of Baghdad in Iraq used a pigeon post system to keep in touch with the far reaches of his empire. By the 1800s carrier pigeons were widely used for sending messages, but the birds have since been replaced by the telegraph, telephone, and radio.

Diesel, Rudolf
Inventor of diesel engine

internal combustion engine engine powered by burning a mixture of fuel and air inside narrow chambers called cylinders

The German engineer Rudolf Diesel invented a type of **internal combustion engine,** which is named after him. Diesel engines are widely used in locomotives, ships, trucks, and some cars.

Born in Paris in 1858, Diesel attended school in Germany, where he excelled in engineering. In 1880 he joined the firm of Carl von Linde, the scientist who invented the modern refrigeration system. In 1890 Diesel developed a plan for an engine that used very hot compressed air to ignite the fuel. He obtained a patent for it two years later. Over the next few years, Diesel built trial models of the engine before producing the first full-scale version in 1897. The simple and durable engine made much more efficient use of its fuel than the steam engines of the day and earned Diesel great wealth. After losing most of his money on poor investments, he disappeared in 1913 during a voyage across the English Channel, possibly by falling overboard. *See also* AUTOMO-BILES, HISTORY OF; ENGINES.

Direction Finding Systems

see *Global Positioning System (GPS); Loran; Navigation.*

Dirigibles

see *Airships.*

Disasters

see *Accidents; Shipwrecks.*

Diving

Diving enables people to move around and explore areas under water. It is a popular sport as well as a valuable technique used in underwater construction, **salvage** operations, and research.

Development of Diving Techniques. The earliest form of diving was free diving. Since ancient times, people have ventured beneath the waves to gather fish, pearls, and sponges or to search for the remains of sunken ships. One improvement to free diving was a short breathing tube called a snorkel, which allowed a person to swim along the surface, drawing air from above. Diving to greater depths was limited by the length of time an individual could stay under water without breathing, usually about one minute.

To overcome this obstacle, people began experimenting with methods to supply divers with air. Medieval divers employed diving bells, large structures open at the bottom. When lowered into the water, open end first, the bell kept air trapped inside. In 1715 John Lethbridge of England invented a waterproof leather suit that covered the diver's head and body. The suit held enough air for a 30-minute stay under water. By 1830 Augustus Siebe of Germany had developed a leather suit with a metal and glass helmet and a pump to supply air from the surface.

Later engineers pursued the idea that divers could carry their own supply of air. They created scuba systems—a name formed from the first letters of the words *self-contained underwater breathing apparatus.* The first reliable scuba system—the Aqua Lung—was developed in 1943 by French naval officer Jacques-Yves Cousteau and Émile Gagnan, an engineer. The Aqua Lung includes metal tanks containing a mixture of oxygen and other gases, worn on the back. Divers breathe the gas through a short hose equipped with a demand regulator, a device that opens the flow when they inhale.

salvage *saving or recovering property lost underwater*

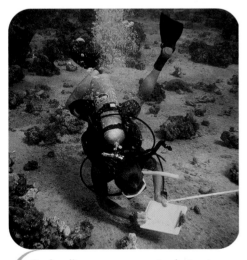

Scuba divers use oxygen tanks to stay underwater for an extended period. Besides recreational exploration, divers' activities include such work as studying marine organisms, repairing underwater structures, and conducting environmental research.

atmospheric pressure pressure exerted by the Earth's atmosphere at any given point on the planet's surface

Hazards of Diving.

A deep-water diver faces many dangers. Most obvious is the risk of running out of air. Changes in **atmospheric pressure** can also present a serious problem. The human body is accustomed to the weight of the atmosphere at the Earth's surface, a quantity called one atmosphere. The pressure of water on the diver's body increases by one atmosphere for about every 30 feet of depth.

Increasing pressure forces air to be absorbed by the diver's bloodstream and body tissues. As the diver heads back to the surface, these gases are released again. If the ascent occurs too quickly, the gases form bubbles in the bloodstream that can cause serious injury or death. This condition, known as decompression sickness, or the bends, can be avoided by rising to the surface slowly and in stages.

Diving with Vehicles.

Diving vehicles, also called submersibles, can protect humans from the cold temperatures and severe pressure of the ocean's depths. The bathysphere, invented in 1930, was a steel sphere that could be lowered into the water on a long cable. It was followed in 1948 by the bathyscaphe, a propeller-driven diving vehicle with a watertight cabin. Modern submersibles, built to withstand huge amounts of water pressure, can descend to depths as great as 20,000 feet (6,100 m)—much deeper than a lone diver can tolerate. *See also* ATMOSPHERIC PRESSURE; HEALTH ISSUES; SUBMARINES AND SUBMERSIBLES.

Docks

see Harbors and Ports.

DOT

see Transportation, U.S. Department of.

Drive-Ins

Drive-in establishments enable customers to remain outside in their cars while conducting business or receiving service. Fast-food restaurants and banks are the most common drive-ins in the United States.

Drive-ins appeared in the United States in the 1920s and 1930s, when thousands of fast-food stands sprang up at the edges of towns around the country. The first of them, Royce Hailey's Pig Stand, opened in Dallas, Texas, in 1921.

Most drive-in stands offered hamburgers, hot dogs, sodas, and milk shakes. Customers stayed in their cars, while carhops—usually teenagers—took their orders and brought their food on trays. Many drive-in food stands closed during the winter months.

The drive-in movie theater appeared in 1933 near Camden, New Jersey. People drove to a parking area and stayed in their cars to watch a movie on a large outdoor screen. By the late 1950s the United States had about 4,000 drive-in movies, but television cut into their popularity and few remain today.

Other drive-in businesses have thrived. Thousands of fast-food restaurants around the country now have drive-through service, as do many banks and some grocery stores and drugstores. Drive-through businesses can stay open year-round. *See also* Automobiles, Effects of; Service Stations.

Driving

Further Information
To learn more about accidents, insurance, motor vehicles, and roads, see the related articles listed at the end of this entry.

The ability to drive enables people to travel from place to place whenever they wish. It also provides a convenient way of moving passengers and baggage. As a result, driving has become an important part of modern life. The United States has about 180 million licensed drivers. Hundreds of millions of other drivers take to the road each day throughout the rest of the world.

Drivers and Driving

Operating a car, truck, or bus is a complex and demanding task. Drivers must be continuously aware of traffic regulations, road conditions, and other vehicles around them. Anyone who gets behind the wheel—from a teenager just learning to drive to a professional bus or truck driver—has an obligation to understand the rules of the road and practice safe driving habits. Failing to act responsibly can endanger lives. The courts have established that driving is not a right but a privilege that can be withdrawn.

Age and Gender. In the United States, more than half of all drivers are between 25 and 50 years old. Almost all states have a minimum driving age of 16 or 17 years and restrict when and where the youngest drivers can operate a vehicle. Although teenagers make up only about 5 percent of the licensed drivers in the country, they are involved in about four times as many fatal car accidents as older drivers. According to safety experts, the high collision rate of this age group may be the result of lack of experience and the tendency to take greater risks than older people.

About 9 percent of drivers in the United States are over age 70. Despite many years of behind-the-wheel experience, this group also has a high accident rate. As people age, their eyesight, hearing, physical coordination, and reaction time may decline, diminishing driving skills.

At all age levels, the number of male and female drivers in the United States is about equal, with men outnumbering women only slightly. However, far more men than women earn a living by driving—operating vehicles such as trucks, buses, taxis, and race cars—and men are involved in twice as many car fatalities as women.

Driver Education. Driving is not an inborn skill but must be learned. It requires studying traffic rules and regulations as well as behind-the-wheel practice. Many young people first learn to drive from parents or other relatives. But the best way to learn is with a qualified driving instructor.

Numerous high schools in the United States offer driver education programs for students. First organized by the American Automobile

Local police and state highway patrols enforce traffic and safety laws along roads throughout the United States. Traffic violations such as exceeding the speed limit or ignoring a stop sign often lead to traffic tickets.

Association (AAA) in the mid-1930s, such programs have trained millions of young people over the years. High school driver education generally includes both classroom instruction and actual driving practice, allowing students to learn fundamental rules and responsibilities while sharpening their skills.

Commercial driving schools teach beginning drivers as well. They may also provide retraining for experienced drivers. Motorists who are involved in numerous accidents or who consistently violate traffic laws are sometimes required to attend driving classes for retraining.

Licensing Drivers. Every state requires drivers to have a license to operate a motor vehicle. People who drive carelessly and break traffic rules run the risk of losing their licenses.

In some cases individuals must hold a learner's permit—a restricted operator's license—before they can apply for a standard driver's license. The permit allows practice driving, accompanied by an adult with a regular license.

To get a standard driver's license, applicants must pass a vision test, a written test, and a driving test. The standard license is valid for passenger cars, light trucks, and a number of noncommercial vehicles. In most states specialized licenses are required to operate buses, large trucks, and other commercial vehicles as well as motorcycles.

Many states have introduced graduated licensing programs, which include an intermediate license between the learner's permit and unrestricted driving privileges. Such programs provide additional training and practice time for new drivers and often include more than one road test.

Professional Drivers. Most drivers spend only a small part of the day on the road—commuting to work, running errands, visiting friends, or traveling for business or pleasure. Some individuals, however, earn their living as drivers, either self-employed or working for others.

Professional drivers play a major role in mass transportation and in the trucking industry. Their jobs may involve driving urban or regional buses, large commercial trucks and delivery vans, taxi cabs, limousines, or airport shuttles. A small number of people work as professional race car drivers.

Commercial bus and truck drivers operate large, complex vehicles, and they need special skills. Moreover, those who drive buses, taxis, or limousines are responsible for the safety of their passengers. For these reasons, states often pass specific regulations for these drivers and require them to obtain special licenses.

Driving Safely

Motor vehicle crashes are the leading cause of accidental death in the United States, with at least 40,000 deaths and roughly 2 million injuries each year. Worldwide, an estimated 300,000 people are killed annually in motor vehicle accidents. About two-thirds of all motor vehicle collisions are caused by unsafe or careless drivers.

Although road safety is largely the responsibility of drivers, highway conditions and other factors also play a role. Over the years governments have adopted standards of safety that motor vehicles must meet. The installation of equipment such as seat belts and air bags has helped protect drivers and passengers.

Driving Hazards and Accidents. Because of their power and speed, motor vehicles can pose a serious danger to drivers, passengers, and other motorists on the highway. Mechanical problems, such as failed brakes or tire blowouts, can send a car out of control. Many states require periodic motor vehicle inspections to help prevent such failures. Drivers can also reduce the likelihood of mechanical breakdowns by having their vehicles serviced regularly.

Poorly designed and maintained roads and highways can be hazardous as well. Roads that are improperly "banked" may increase the chance of a vehicle skidding off the road as it travels around curves. Bumping over ruts and potholes—or swerving to avoid them—can cause a motorist to lose control. Inadequate lane markings may lead a driver to drift toward oncoming or passing traffic. Highway authorities can eliminate such hazards through careful road design and timely repairs.

Bad weather is another factor that can make driving treacherous. High winds, ice, snow, and heavy rain all create conditions that may require drivers to decrease speed and proceed with extra caution. Likewise, a thin layer of water and oil on road surfaces may cause a vehicle to slide, a condition known as hydroplaning. Good tires and properly functioning windshield wipers are essential in these circumstances.

One of the greatest safety hazards in driving is alcohol. Driving and drinking do not mix. Alcohol slows a driver's reflexes, impairs vision and judgment, and reduces alertness and concentration. The use of illegal drugs can have similar effects. Alcohol-related accidents account for about 40 percent of all traffic fatalities, and about 20 percent of drivers aged 15 to 20 killed in crashes are intoxicated. The problem of alcohol

An increase in traffic during certain periods, such as the morning and evening rush hours, has led to more aggressive driving styles and an increase in accidents.

use by motorists has led to the formation of organizations such as Mothers Against Drunk Driving (MADD). Their efforts have contributed to a reduction in driving-related deaths since 1982.

Traffic Control. Traffic control devices and regulations are important elements in safe driving. Traffic control devices include road signs and signals that direct the flow of cars and warn drivers of hazards. Road signs give speed limits, provide directions for motorists, and tell them when to stop or yield to merging traffic. Traffic signals indicate when motorists may proceed through intersections. Many countries use standard colors, shapes, and markings for traffic devices. Stop signs in the United States, for example, have a red background and are octagonal, or eight-sided. Such uniformity allows motorists to respond quickly and consistently.

Traffic regulations are another essential part of traffic control. They cover most aspects of driving, including traffic speed, use of lights, passing, stopping, and parking. The laws generally apply throughout a particular locality, but some—such as parking rules—may change during periods of the day or week when traffic is heavier or lighter than usual.

Local police and state highway patrols play a major role in traffic control. Responsible for enforcing traffic regulations, they also provide help in emergencies, direct traffic at the scene of accidents, assist drivers in distress, and patrol roadways to check on travel conditions. Because of a shortage of police in relation to the number of drivers and vehicles on the highways, enforcement of traffic laws is sometimes difficult.

Effective traffic control is increasingly important as growing numbers of vehicles crowd streets and highways. Road congestion and gridlock—a traffic jam that brings movement to a halt—raise the cost of transportation and contribute to air pollution. They can also cause accidents as drivers become frustrated and angry while waiting to proceed. Although great improvements have been made in traffic control, better methods will be required to meet the driving needs of the future. ***See also*** ACCIDENTS; AUTOMOBILES; BUSES; COMMUTING; INSURANCE; MOTORCYCLES; RACE CARS; REGULATION OF TRANSPORTATION; ROADS; TAXIS; TRUCKING INDUSTRY; TRUCKS.

Earhart, Amelia
American aviator

The American aviator Amelia Earhart made several record-setting flights during the 1930s. She became one of the world's best-known pilots and used her prominence to promote women's involvement in flying. Her fame today rests on these achievements and on the mystery surrounding her disappearance over the Pacific Ocean.

Born July 24, 1897, in Atchison, Kansas, Earhart learned to fly in California. When she was working in Boston in 1928, pilot Bill Stultz invited her to accompany him on a flight across the Atlantic Ocean. Earhart gained considerable publicity as the first woman to fly across the ocean—even though she was a passenger, not the pilot.

Earhart made a career of flying and helped found the Ninety-Nines, an association for women pilots. In 1931 she married George Putnam, a

Amelia Earhart set many records in the world of aviation. She was the first woman to fly alone across the Atlantic Ocean, across the United States, and from Hawaii to the U.S. mainland.

publisher. She wrote three books about her flying experiences that did much to create interest in her flights.

After setting several women's airspeed records, Earhart made headlines again in 1932 when she flew alone across the Atlantic—completing that flight as well in record time. In recognition of her achievement, the U.S. Congress awarded her the Distinguished Flying Cross medal. She was the first woman to receive this honor. In the mid-1930s Earhart added two more records to her list of accomplishments: she was the first woman to fly back and forth across the United States and the first person to fly from Hawaii to the U.S. mainland.

The aviator launched her most ambitious effort in 1937, an eastward flight around the world with navigator Fred Noonan. The trip went well for 40 days and 22,000 miles, until the pair reached the Pacific Ocean. Several hours after leaving New Guinea, Earhart reported by radio that she was running low on fuel. No further communications were ever received from her.

A massive search failed to find the aviators or their plane, and the rumors and speculations about their fate have not yet ended. Some people believe that Earhart was captured while spying on Japanese bases in the Pacific. Others report finding traces of her plane on a small island. Nothing is known for certain about her death, but Earhart's influence lives on. Her example inspired many women to become pilots, leading to the formation of the women's flying corps in the U.S. military during World War II. *See also* Aviation, History of.

Electric Cars

Electric cars are vehicles with electric motors powered by rechargeable batteries. First developed in the 1890s, they became quite popular during the early days of the automobile. Electric cars were largely replaced by gasoline-powered cars. But in the 1960s concern over pollution and limited oil supplies led to a renewed interest in using electricity to run cars.

Early Models. The development of electric cars took place in both Europe and the United States. William Morrison of Iowa built one of the first models in 1891. A few years later Henry G. Morris and Pedro G. Salom created the "Electrobat," which served as a taxicab in New York City. A French electric created a sensation in 1898 when it reached a speed of nearly 40 miles per hour (64 km per hour). Another French car surpassed that record the following year, hitting 65 miles per hour (105 km per hour).

Electric cars soon became very popular in the United States, competing successfully with other motor vehicles. By 1900, 38 percent of the automobiles in the United States ran on electric batteries. About 40 percent were powered by steam and 22 percent by gasoline engines. Electrics hit their peak in 1912, when Americans owned nearly 34,000 electric models.

Battery-powered cars had several advantages over steam and gasoline. They were quiet, clean, and odorless, easy to start, and simple to operate. Women in particular liked the comfort, cleanliness, and ease of driving an electric car.

However, these vehicles cost much more to build and operate than gasoline-powered cars. In addition, the heavy weight of the batteries made electric cars much less efficient than gasoline cars. The best models could travel only 50 to 80 miles (80 to 129 km)—under ideal conditions—before their batteries needed recharging. Electric motors also had less power than gasoline engines. Manufacturers of gasoline-powered autos moved decisively ahead when they introduced electric ignition systems that eliminated the unreliable hand cranks used to start their vehicles. In the 1920s few electric cars were left on the streets, though electric buses remained in use in European cities for some time.

Modern Electric Cars. Interest in electric cars was renewed in the 1960s with the growing concern about air pollution and the dwindling supply of the world's petroleum. Scientists, engineers, and auto companies began new research on electric batteries, fuel cell electric generators, and vehicles. Since then various experimental electric cars have been produced, and several models are out on the highways. Some manufacturers are focusing on hybrid vehicles, which combine electric batteries with small gasoline motors or solar cells to charge the batteries.

Yet modern electric cars still suffer many of the same disadvantages as early models—limited travel range, relatively poor performance, and greater expense. Current models need to be recharged about every 100 miles (161 km), and their top speed is about 60 miles per hour (97 km per hour). Until such problems are overcome, electric cars will likely remain a novelty. *See also* AUTOMOBILES, EFFECTS OF; AUTOMOBILES, HISTORY OF; AUTOMOBILES, TYPES OF; ENGINES; VINTAGE CARS.

Electric cars powered solely by batteries can travel only limited distances at moderate speeds. However, engineers are developing hybrid cars, with both electric and gasoline engines, which switch to gasoline power at high speeds.

Electric Motors

see Engines.

Electric Trains

see Railway Trains, Parts of; Railway Trains, Types of.

Elevated Railways

see Subways.

Elevators and Escalators

Elevators and escalators are mechanical devices that move people and freight from one floor of a building to another. In use throughout the world, they have become indispensable for carrying passengers and goods up or down.

Elevators. An elevator is basically a platform, or car, that travels from one level to another. Ancient peoples used cables and pulleys to raise and lower wooden platforms. Operated by human or animal power, these lifts were particularly valuable in construction.

In the early 1800s people began using **hydraulic** and steam power to raise elevator cars loaded with freight. Though definitely an improvement over traditional methods, the new devices moved slowly and the supporting ropes broke frequently. In 1853 an American inventor, Elisha Otis, introduced an automatic safety device to prevent elevator cars from falling if a rope broke. This invention led to the development of the modern passenger elevator.

The first steam-powered passenger elevator was installed in a department store in New York City in 1857, and electric-powered elevators appeared by the 1880s. Like modern elevators, these models consisted of an enclosed car and steel frame guided along rails within a vertical shaft.

Some elevators use a hydraulic system to raise and lower the car. These do not have cables. The elevator is raised and lowered by a **piston** that moves up and down inside a cylinder deep underground. When a pump fills the cylinder with fluid, the pressure forces the piston and the car upward. When fluid exits the cylinder through a valve, the elevator descends. Hydraulic elevators travel slowly, and the difficulty of drilling a deep cylinder limits their use to buildings of less than ten stories.

The majority of modern elevators have traction systems—either geared or gearless—which depend on steel cables to raise and lower the car. One end of a cable is attached to the top of the car. The other end goes to the top of the shaft, over a pulley called a sheave, and down to a heavy counterweight that balances the weight of the car. The sheave is driven by an electric motor.

Geared elevators have a gear to transmit the energy of the spinning sheave to the cables. The gear slows the elevator, making it useful in

hydraulic operated by or using water or other liquids in motion

piston mechanical part moved back and forth by fluid pressure inside a chamber

Gearless Elevator

Control system

Drive system

Governor

Hoisting cables

Door operator

Car

Car safety devices

Traveling cable

Counterweight

Guide rails

Car guide rail

Buffer

Modern gearless elevators are equipped with traction systems and sets of cables to raise and lower the individual cars.

conveyor mechanical device for moving articles on a belt or chain from one place to another

residential buildings of moderate height. However, gears can wear down and make noise. Gearless elevators, which provide a smoother, quieter, faster ride, are preferred for tall buildings.

Most modern elevators are automatic, equipped with computers and sensors that control the cars and their doors. Millions of passengers and tons of freight travel on elevators every day, making them an important part of urban transportation. In fact, city skyscrapers would not have been possible without modern elevators.

Escalators. Escalators are open, moving stairways that transport a steady flow of people from one level to another. First built in the United States in the 1890s, they operate in airports, subway stations, stores, malls, hotels, and many other buildings.

An escalator is a type of **conveyor** powered by an electric motor. Attached to the conveyor belt are steps that run on wheels along the tracks of a steel frame, or truss. The wheels are pulled by heavy metal chains that move around large gears at the top and bottom of the escalator. Enclosing the steps are protective walls, called balustrades, topped by moving handrails that travel at the same speed as the steps. The steps flatten out at both ends of the escalator, enabling passengers to get on and off easily. The movement of an escalator can be reversed so that the escalator travels either up or down.

Varying in speed, length, and width, escalators can carry from 5,000 to 10,000 individuals per hour. They usually rise at an angle of 30 degrees. Two of the world's highest escalators take pedestrians up and down to a tunnel that lies 85 feet (26 m) below the Tyne River in England. ***See also*** CONVEYORS; PEOPLE MOVERS.

Emergency Transportation

civilian nonmilitary

Emergency transportation provides health and rescue services to people in life-threatening situations. With a variety of vehicles on land, sea, and air, emergency transportation plays a vital role in modern health care.

Ambulances. The history of the ambulance began in France in the 1700s when horse-drawn wagons carried wounded soldiers from battlefields to medical areas behind the lines. Some ambulances had springs to smooth the trip for patients and prevent further injury over rough roads or fields.

The first **civilian** ambulances entered service in the mid-1800s. The Commercial Hospital in Cincinnati, Ohio, started using carriages to transport sick and injured patients before 1865. In 1878 a group in England organized an ambulance service. Motorized ambulances first appeared in France in 1895 and gradually replaced horse-drawn vehicles in most areas.

Early ambulances transported people to hospitals but carried little medical equipment. Ambulance workers provided almost no medical care until the 1970s, when they started treating patients inside the ambulance. Most emergency vehicles carry a broad array of equipment, including bandages, oxygen masks, medications, and monitors. Ambulance workers, known as emergency medical technicians (EMTs) or paramedics, are highly trained medical professionals. In addition to applying emergency treatment, EMTs stay in contact with hospital doctors during the trip to convey information and receive advice.

Modern ambulances are specially designed vehicles, usually equipped with sirens and flashing lights to warn of their approach.

Most are owned and operated by hospitals and by professional or volunteer ambulance services in local communities.

Lifeboats. People have used boats to rescue people at sea for centuries. In the late 1700s, the British began to build vessels specifically designed to serve as lifeboats. The early models focused on **buoyancy** and stability, and some were proclaimed to be unsinkable. Modern lifeboats are often fitted with small engines, radio communications, medical supplies, food, flares, ropes, searchlights, and other vital resources. All ships carry their own lifeboats or life rafts that are kept supplied and ready to launch at any moment.

Lifeboats and other vessels may also patrol coastal waters, available to save sailors shipwrecked offshore. Britain and the United States led the way in establishing coast guards, and many countries today have a **maritime** agency assigned to rescue operations.

buoyancy force that exerts an upward push on an object

maritime related to the sea or shipping

Ambulances, helicopters, and marine rescue teams provide emergency transportation and assistance. In this photo, rescue workers lift an accident victim aboard a helicopter.

The Red Cross

The International Red Cross was formed in Europe to provide medical care to wounded soldiers in 1863. The organization spread around the world—the U.S. Civil War inspired Clara Barton to petition Congress for an American branch of the Red Cross. Today more than 100 national Red Cross societies and two international ones are joined by the Red Crescent in Arab countries and the Red Star of David in Israel. These societies call on many land, sea, and air vehicles—as well as dedicated personnel—to take part in relief efforts around the world.

Helicopters. Since the 1950s helicopters have proved their worth in battles, natural disasters, and other emergencies. They saved many lives by evacuating wounded U.S. soldiers in the Korean War and the Vietnam War. Modern armed forces and the U.S. Coast Guard maintain fleets of helicopters that are often used for rescue operations. Some rescue helicopters operate from ships.

Helicopters have also become crucial vehicles in civilian rescue operations. Capable of flying to almost any spot, they can hover over the site and lower ropes, ladders, harnesses, and even medical personnel to people in distress. Helicopters have saved people from sinking ships, burning buildings, raging floodwaters, and hard-to-reach areas in the backwoods or mountains. In high-traffic urban regions, helicopters can sometimes transport patients to hospitals much faster than an ambulance. They can also deliver food and medical supplies to places that cannot be reached by other vehicles.

EMS Systems. Many cities and communities maintain ambulances and other emergency vehicles as part of emergency medical services (EMS) systems. These highly organized networks of medical care facilities and trained personnel can provide emergency treatment and transport with speed and efficiency. In the United States, EMS systems can be accessed by dialing a special telephone number, usually 9-1-1. EMS systems save many thousands of lives each year. *See also* ACCIDENTS; COAST GUARD; HELICOPTERS; SHIPS AND BOATS, SAFETY OF.

Energy

People around the world use energy to heat or cool homes; light buildings; operate tools and computers; and provide power for industry. In addition, the forms of transportation used in modern societies—automobiles, trains, ships, and airplanes—consume enormous amounts of energy. As human populations expand and the demand for energy grows, some major energy sources are becoming scarce. Moreover, their use has contributed to air and water pollution and various other environmental problems. One of the greatest challenges for the future will be to develop new sources of energy that are abundant, relatively inexpensive, and not harmful to humans or the environment.

Demand for Energy

Throughout most of early human history, muscle power was the only available source of energy. Over time people learned to use fire and animal power and to harness the energy of the wind and moving water with sails, windmills, and waterwheels. Early land transportation was limited to animal-drawn carts or wagons and, of course, walking. Sails and oars powered ships and boats on the world's rivers, lakes, and seas.

Although fossil fuels such as coal, petroleum, and natural gas were discovered hundreds or even thousands of years ago, humans lacked the technology to use them efficiently until fairly recently. In the 1700s coal became important as a power source for machines and factories in

England, contributing to the nation's shift from an agricultural to an industrial economy.

The greatest increases in energy use have occurred within the last 100 years, much of them in industrialized societies. The United States, for example, consumed about 400 times more electricity in the 1990s than it did in 1900. Industrialized nations use much more energy than less developed societies—and a much higher proportion of energy for transportation. The world's growing demand for energy will eventually exceed the supplies of many types of fuels. But a number of alternatives are being developed that may provide new sources of power.

Wood and Fossil Fuels

The most common sources of energy are wood and fossil fuels—substances that developed over millions of years as dead plant matter changed form under intense heat and pressure. Burning these fuels releases energy stored within the plant matter. Coal, petroleum, and natural gas are the most important fossil fuels. They provide about 90 percent of all the energy used in the world today.

Wood. People have burned wood for thousands of years to cook food, dry bricks, bake pottery, and heat homes. It has not been important as an energy source for transportation, although it was used as a fuel in early railroad locomotives.

Coal. The most abundant fossil fuel is coal, a solid rocklike substance usually found in layers under the surface of the Earth. The ancient

Between 1950 and 1995 the amount of petroleum used in transportation tripled. Petroleum use by electric utilities and industry also increased enormously, but residential and commercial consumption remained fairly constant.

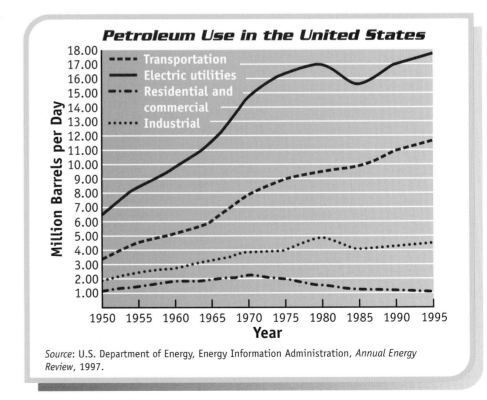

Petroleum Use in the United States

Source: U.S. Department of Energy, Energy Information Administration, *Annual Energy Review*, 1997.

Chinese burned coal for heating and cooking before 1000 B.C. Mined in Europe by the A.D. 1100s, the mineral became a major source of energy during the Industrial Revolution that began in the 1700s. During the 1800s coal was the main fuel for steam engines that drove both ships and locomotives. It remained their primary source of energy until the invention of diesel engines in the early 1900s.

Today coal provides about 28 percent of the world's energy and about 23 percent of the energy needs of the United States. Most coal in the United States is used for generating electricity and in the manufacture of steel, an important material in the construction of many forms of transportation. A major problem with coal is that it releases various **pollutants** into the air when it is burned.

Petroleum and Natural Gas. These fuels often occur together in deposits within the Earth. The petroleum in underground reservoirs is a thick liquid called crude oil. Although crude oil will burn and produce heat, it is usually put through a refining process to convert it into specific forms, such as gasoline, jet fuel, or heating oil. Most petroleum is converted into fuels for transportation. Nearly all automobiles and trucks burn gasoline or diesel fuel; most ships and trains use diesel fuel.

Petroleum furnishes about 40 percent of the world's energy and about 43 percent of the energy needs of the United States. However, like coal, petroleum products release pollutants into the air when they are burned. In fact, **combustion** of gasoline in cars and other motor vehicles is one of the greatest sources of air pollution. Many scientists believe that the use of fossil fuels is a major factor contributing to a gradual warming of the Earth's atmosphere.

Natural gas provides about 21 percent of the world's energy and 23 percent of that used in the United States. A clean source of energy, it does not need refining and does not harm the environment. However, deposits of natural gas—like those of all fossil fuels—are limited. Pipelines usually carry the fuel directly to distributors and consumers. Few vehicles use natural gas as a fuel, though an increasing number of cars and trucks are being converted to do so for environmental reasons.

Companies use offshore platforms to drill for oil in bodies of water such as the Gulf of Mexico.

pollutant *something that contaminates the environment*

combustion *process of burning*

Wind Power and Waterpower

For centuries people relied on the wind to propel sailing ships used for travel, commerce, and exploration. Windmills, which appeared in Europe as early as the 1200s, harnessed the power of wind to do work. Wind-powered sailing ships still serve as transportation in some parts of the world, but in the United States they are used mostly for recreation.

Waterpower, another important source of energy throughout history, has had a limited role in transportation. Early people learned how to use the power of moving water to operate waterwheels. They also relied on the force of the current to float along waterways in rafts and other flatboats. Waterpower carried boatloads of passengers and cargo swiftly downstream on rivers. Traveling upstream was much harder until the invention of steamboats.

Nuclear Energy

Nuclear energy has the potential for supplying an almost limitless amount of power. This power is produced by two types of nuclear reactions: fission and fusion. In fission the atoms of certain elements are split apart, releasing heat and **radiation.** The same type of process is used to cause atomic explosions. But in nuclear power plants the reaction is controlled so that the energy that is released can be used. Such plants currently produce about 6 percent of the world's energy.

The engines of some aircraft carriers and submarines are powered by nuclear reactors. These vessels can run for years without refueling. But nuclear power plants produce waste products—including quantities of hot water—that may damage the environment. Radioactive materials generated by the reactors remain dangerous for long periods, and the safe disposal of these wastes has become a major concern.

In nuclear fusion, atoms collide with such force that they fuse, or join together, producing enormous amounts of heat in the process. Scientists do not yet know how to control this type of nuclear reaction, so it is not available as a source of energy. It holds great potential for the future, however. Nuclear fusion can be produced with forms of hydrogen, the most abundant element on Earth, and the waste products of fusion are not dangerous.

Alternative Energy Sources and Fuels

Various alternative energy sources and fuels offer possibilities for providing more power in the future. Some are already in use, while others are still experimental. Many of these energy sources are attractive because they cause little harm to the environment.

Solar power—energy released by the Sun—is nonpolluting and limitless. The problem is to concentrate, use, and store this energy efficiently and economically. Solar energy can be collected in devices called solar cells, which convert the energy into electricity inefficiently. Small solar cells provide energy for items such as calculators and watches. Larger ones can be used to power experimental automobiles. Despite its advantages, solar energy is still too expensive and inefficient for large-scale use in transportation.

Another alternative energy source is biomass—organic matter including plants and all solid and liquid wastes such as garbage and sewage. The burning of biomass produces heat, which can be used to

radiation *tiny, harmful particles of matter given off during a nuclear reaction*

Boosting Energy Output

Scientists are studying ways to use fossil fuels more efficiently. One approach involves magnetohydrodynamic generators, devices that burn fuel at very high temperatures and convert it into hot electrified gas. The gas is forced through a powerful magnetic field, which produces an electric current that can be directed into power lines. Using this method can significantly increase the amount of energy produced by coal. However, numerous technical problems must be overcome before these generators can be used on a wide scale.

generate electricity. Through a process called bioconversion, engineers can change biomass into liquid and gaseous fuels, such as methanol, gasohol, and methane gas. Automobiles can use some of these fuels as a source of power.

Improved Efficiency and Conservation

Scientists and engineers are working to develop more efficient methods of recovering and using fossil fuels and other sources of energy and to improve alternative forms of energy. The development of nonpolluting energy sources is a high priority in order to safeguard the environment and important natural resources.

Conservation is one way of increasing efficiency and lessening the impact of energy use on the environment. Changing transportation habits can help reduce energy consumption. People can save energy by switching to more fuel-efficient cars, walking instead of driving whenever possible, and traveling on buses or other forms of mass transportation instead of in private vehicles. Conserving energy and developing new and more efficient power sources will be crucial to meet the energy needs of the future. *See also* AIR CURRENT AND WIND; AUTOMOBILES: RELATED INDUSTRIES; ELECTRIC CARS; ENGINES; HEALTH ISSUES; HORSEPOWER; PIPELINES; POLLUTION AND TRANSPORTATION.

Engines

propulsion process of driving or propelling

Further Information
To learn more about the vehicles propelled by different types of engines, see the related articles listed at the end of this entry.

The invention of the engine—a device that converts energy from fuel into mechanical force and motion—revolutionized transportation. Before the arrival of engines, people depended on wind, animal, or human power for transportation. These methods were slow and unreliable and could carry limited loads.

In the 1700s steam engines became available, providing an efficient source of **propulsion** that worked day in and day out. Steam-powered ships and carriages could move faster and carry more cargo than ever before. During the next two centuries, different types of engines made possible entirely new forms of transportation, such as railroads, automobiles, and airplanes. Today, a wide variety of engine-powered vehicles carry passengers and freight all over the world.

Steam Engines

In 1712 English inventor Thomas Newcomen developed the first commercially successful steam engine to pump water from mines. More than 50 years later the Scottish inventor James Watt redesigned this crude engine, creating what was essentially the modern steam engine, in which a piston delivers power to a rotating shaft. However, both the Newcomen and Watt engines were too large and heavy to mount on a vehicle, and they were used only on stationary equipment.

Steam engines operating at higher pressures than Watt's were needed to power carriages and boats. In 1798 English inventor Richard

In a steam engine, steam is converted into mechanical energy that powers vehicles and machines.

Steam Engine

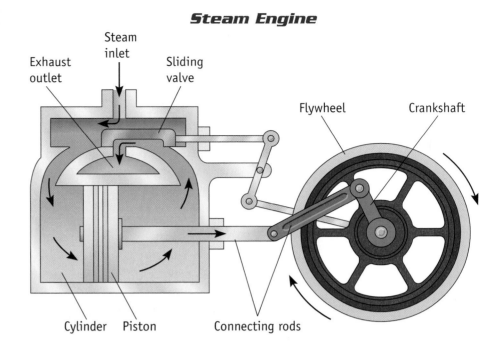

Steam inlet

Exhaust outlet

Sliding valve

Flywheel

Crankshaft

Cylinder   Piston

Connecting rods

Trevithick developed a relatively high-pressure steam engine that he used to drive steam carriages on roads. In 1804 his engine provided energy for the first crude railroad locomotive. The first ship equipped with a steam engine was the experimental French-made *Pyroscaphe,* demonstrated in 1783. In 1807 American inventor Robert Fulton began a new era in water transportation with the first commercially successful steamboat, the *Clermont.*

Steam Engine Operation.
Steam engines are external combustion engines, meaning that they burn fuel outside the engine. The burning fuel heats water in a boiler, a large tank partly filled with water. The boiling water produces steam, which builds up pressure as more heat is applied under the boiler. The pressure eventually provides the energy to run the engine and do work.

Steam from the boiler is piped to a closed container called a steam chest. A sliding valve inside the steam chest opens an **intake** to let the steam pass into a cylinder containing a **piston.** Both the valve and the piston are attached to a **flywheel** by means of connecting rods.

Steam rushing into one end of the cylinder pushes against the piston and forces it to the other end of the cylinder. As the piston moves, it turns the flywheel, which causes the valve to close the intake. At the same time, the valve opens an exhaust outlet, and the piston pushes spent steam out of the cylinder through the outlet. As the piston reaches the other end of the cylinder, the valve opens an intake at that end. Steam flows in and the cycle is repeated.

In order for a steam engine to turn wheels or propellers, the piston's back and forth motion must be converted to a circular motion. That is the function of the crankshaft, a shaft with a U-shaped bend that is linked to the piston by a connecting rod. The connecting rod moves back and forth with the piston, but the U-shaped bend causes the crankshaft to rotate.

intake opening through which fluid enters a container

piston mechanical part moved back and forth by fluid pressure inside a chamber

flywheel heavy wheel used to reduce variations in the speed of a machine

Age of Steam. By the early 1830s high-pressure steam engines had been greatly improved, and the first practical steam-powered railroads were built. Steam-powered ships began to replace sailing ships after the 1850s, and by the late 1800s successful steam-powered cars were being built. But as popular as they were, steam engines did have drawbacks. The equipment was bulky and heavy, and the engine used fuel inefficiently. The best steam engines converted only about 12 percent of the fuel energy to mechanical power. Gasoline engines, which eventually replaced steam engines for various uses, convert as much as 28 percent. Diesel engines—which can make use of up to 35 percent of their fuel energy—are even more efficient.

Gasoline Engines

Relative to their weight, gasoline engines produce a larger amount of power than steam engines. Their high output, light weight, and compact size have made them ideal power plants for self-propelled vehicles, particularly automobiles, light trucks, and certain aircraft.

Because gasoline engines get their power by burning fuel inside the engine, they are called internal combustion engines. French inventor Jean-Joseph-Etienne Lenoir built the first practical internal combustion engine in 1859, a one-cylinder motor that used coal gas. He succeeded in powering a carriage with it, but his engine was crude and inefficient.

In 1876 the German inventor Nikolaus Otto built the first four-stroke internal combustion engine, a smooth-running, highly efficient engine that closely resembled the modern gasoline engine. Otto sold some 50,000 models, and the success of his engine helped bring an end to the steam age. From the early 1900s onward, automobile makers favored four-stroke engines for their cars. Because of their high power output, these engines were used to run airplanes in the early years of aviation.

The two basic types of gasoline engines in use today are reciprocating and rotary. Reciprocating engines have pistons that move up and down in cylinders, while the newer rotary engines have a triangular rotor that spins inside the combustion chamber.

Reciprocating Engines. These engines work by drawing a mixture of fuel and air into a cylinder that contains a piston. The piston compresses the mixture, which is then ignited by an electric spark from a spark plug. The resulting explosion forces gases against the piston. As the piston moves downward in the cylinder, it turns a crankshaft, converting the up and down motion to rotation.

The gasoline engines in automobiles are called four-stroke engines because they require four up and down piston movements, or strokes, to turn the crankshaft once. The four movements are the intake, compression, power, and exhaust strokes. During the intake stroke the downward motion of the piston draws the fuel-air mixture into the cylinder. During the compression stroke the piston moves up and compresses the mixture to about one-sixth of its original volume. The spark plug then ignites the

Reining in the Steam Carriages

Steam-powered carriages began to appear on English roads after 1801. But the carriages belched smoke and spat out hot sparks that sometimes set fire to crops and wooden bridges. They also made strange noises that scared horses, which many businesses relied on to transport people and freight. A public outcry led the British Parliament to pass laws to rein in the new vehicles and maintain the supremacy of the horse. One law imposed a 4-mile-per-hour (6.4-km-per-hour) speed limit on steam carriages, while another required that a man waving a red flag walk in front of the carriage. These laws were finally repealed in 1896, when gasoline-powered automobiles were gaining ground.

Most early trains had locomotives with steam engines. However, by the end of the 1800s, these engines were being replaced by electric and diesel models.

mixture, and the resulting explosion forces the piston down, causing the power stroke. During the exhaust stroke the piston moves up, pushing the burned gases out of the cylinder.

Two-stroke engines use fewer movements to turn a crankshaft. First, the upward motion of the piston compresses the fuel-air mixture in the cylinder while drawing fresh mixture into a lower chamber called the crankcase. When the piston is at the top of the cylinder, the fuel is ignited, pushing down the piston and forcing the burned gases out. The fresh fuel mixture enters the cylinder and the process starts again. Two-stroke engines produce less power than four-stroke engines and are generally used in light vehicles, such as small motorcycles.

Rotary Engines. The rotary engine, invented in the 1950s by the German engineer Felix Wankel, has no pistons or valves. Instead, it contains a triangular rotor that turns inside a curved combustion chamber. During the intake phase, the fuel-air mixture enters the space between one side of the rotor and the wall of the combustion chamber. The turning rotor compresses the mixture until it is ignited. Expanding gases then force the rotor to turn until it passes the exhaust port and the gases escape. Each time the rotor makes a full turn, there are three combustion phases, one for each of the three spaces created by the triangular rotor.

This results in smoother operation of the engine at high speeds, an important advantage. The Wankel's few moving parts are another plus. But the engine uses more fuel than a conventional four-stroke engine and gives off more pollutants.

Diesel Engines

German engineer Rudolf Diesel invented yet another type of internal combustion engine, the diesel, which resembles the four-stroke gasoline engine in many ways. However, there are some important differences. During the compression stroke, diesels compress air inside the cylinder to very high pressures, raising the temperature dramatically. Heavy fuel oil is then injected into the cylinder, where the superheated air ignites it—a much simpler ignition system than that used in four-stroke gasoline engines.

Diesels use fuel more efficiently than gasoline engines, and the heavy oil they burn is both safer and cheaper than gasoline. However, they tend to emit high levels of pollutants. Furthermore, diesels need heavy engine blocks to handle the high pressures involved, and this extra weight is a disadvantage in an automobile. Diesel engines, with their low fuel costs, are most often found in heavy-duty vehicles, such as trucks, buses, locomotives, and ships.

Although diesel engines burn fuel more efficiently and cheaply than gasoline engines, they release more pollutants.

Diesel Engine

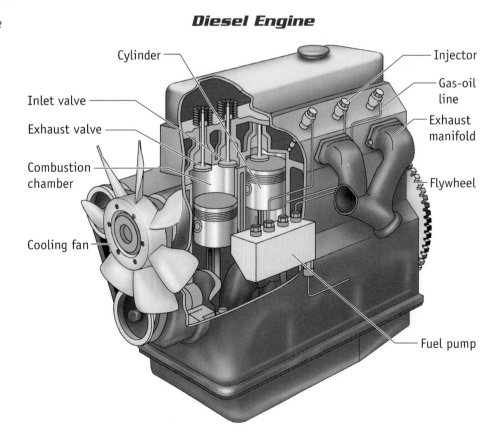

Cylinder

Inlet valve

Exhaust valve

Combustion chamber

Cooling fan

Injector

Gas-oil line

Exhaust manifold

Flywheel

Fuel pump

Electric Motors

Electric motors are common in many household appliances, but their use in vehicles has largely been limited to the diesel-electric engines that power locomotives. In such arrangements, a diesel engine drives an electric generator, which provides the energy for electric motors that turn the locomotive's wheels.

An electric motor operates using two basic principles of physics: opposite poles of a magnet attract while like poles repel, and electric current passing through a wire will create a magnetic field. In a simple electric motor, a wire loop, or rotor, is placed between two magnets. When an electric current passes through the rotor, the rotor becomes magnetized and makes one half-turn until its magnetic poles align with the opposite poles of the magnets. When the current is turned off, then on again, the rotor makes another half-turn. With the current continuously turned on and off, the rotor can be made to spin very quickly. Additional loops of wire in the rotor increase the engine's power. In a locomotive, the rotor is connected to an axle that turns the wheels.

Turbine Engines

Turbine engines can be used to drive wheels, turn ship or airplane propellers, or do other work. The history of turbines goes back to ancient Greece, where waterwheels turned by the flow of a stream were employed to grind grain and press oil from olives. Windmills have been used in the same way since the Middle Ages. However, these open turbines lose much of the energy of the water and wind striking them. The development of modern turbines began in the early 1800s, with the construction of the first enclosed water turbines.

The heart of a turbine engine—like the central part of the electric motor—is called the rotor. The turbine rotor is a wheel with curved blades around its outer edge. Powerful jets of steam or hot gases directed at the blades turn the rotor quickly. The rotor can be attached to an axle to rotate machinery parts.

Steam Turbines.   In 1884 the English inventor Charles Parsons developed a turbine in which steam passed through a series of rotors to extract as much energy as possible. In 1897 he built a ship named the *Turbinia* that was powered with his steam turbines. The vessel raced along at 34.5 knots, an incredible speed at the time, and soon after, naval warships were fitted with Parsons's turbines.

Modern steam turbines may have 50 or more rotors connected to the same shaft and can develop up to 750 million watts of power. Among the most powerful engines, steam turbines are used to propel giant ships and turn large electrical generators.

Gas Turbines.   The first successful gas turbine engines were built during the 1930s. Since then, they have been used in ships, locomotives, buses, and experimental turbine-powered automobiles. Jet engines incorporate basic features of gas turbines.

Gas turbines work at much higher pressure and temperature than steam turbines. Air is drawn into the front of the turbine and forced through a compressor, which raises the pressure by four or five times. The pressurized air rushes from the compressor to the combustion chamber, where fuel is injected and ignited to produce the hot gases that drive the turbine. The turbine and the compressor are connected to the same shaft, so part of the energy produced by a turbine goes toward running the compressor.

Most turbines contain several stages, each consisting of a set of fixed blades and a rotor. The stages get larger in diameter because the gases expand as they flow through the turbine. The fixed blades guide the gases into the rotor's moving blades. Each stage extracts more energy from the hot gases, increasing the engine's power. Many turbines send their exhaust gases to a regenerator, which heats the air being pressurized in the compressor. This process makes the engine more fuel efficient.

Jet Engines

Successful jet engines were developed in the late 1930s by two engineers, Hans von Ohain of Germany and an Englishman named Frank Whittle. Whittle patented a jet engine in 1930, but it was too heavy for use on airplanes. By the end of World War II, however, Whittle was building practical jet engines for aircraft. Ohain, meanwhile, produced his own jet engine, and in 1939 it powered a German-made experimental jet called the Heinkel 178. By the end of the war, the Germans had built jet fighters capable of traveling at 550 miles per hour (885 km per hour). In 1949 the British de Havilland Comet became the first passenger airliner to be propelled by jet engines, and from that time forward the race was on to build bigger, faster jet planes.

The three basic types of jet engines in general use are turbojets, turbofans, and turboprops.

The development of jet engines contributed to the growth of air travel, making long journeys faster and more popular.

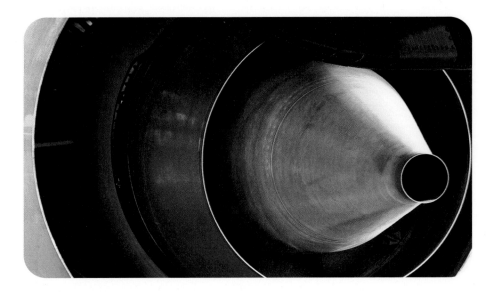

Turbojets.   The turbojet is essentially a gas turbine that operates by sucking in large quantities of air through the open front end of the engine. The air is compressed by a set of bladed wheels and then rushes into the combustion chamber, where it is mixed with kerosene-like fuel and ignited. The explosive combustion forces the expanding gases rearward, producing the thrust that keeps the plane airborne. On the way out of the engine, the gases rotate a turbine that provides the energy to run the engine's compressor. Some jets have an afterburner that injects fuel into the hot exhaust gases after they have passed the turbine but before they reach the open air beyond the engine's exhaust nozzle. The resulting combustion adds considerably to the engine's thrust.

Turbofans and Turboprops.   Turbofans operate in much the same way as turbojets, except that a large fan on the front of the engine pumps extra air into the engine. However, only part of that air goes into the compressor and combustion chamber. The rest is channeled around the engine and out the exhaust in order to add to the engine's thrust. The fan, like the compressor, is driven by a turbine mounted in the stream of hot gases behind the combustion chamber.

A turboprop engine looks much like a turbojet, but the gases rushing out of the combustion chamber pass through turbines, which in turn drive a propeller. Turboprop engines are more efficient than turbojets but cannot achieve the same high speeds. Rotor blades of jet-powered helicopters are turned by turboshaft engines, which are basically turboprop engines mounted vertically. *See also* AIRCRAFT, PARTS OF; AUTOMOBILES, PARTS OF; DIESEL, RUDOLF; ELECTRIC CARS; FULTON, ROBERT; JET PLANES; LENOIR, JEAN-JOSEPH-ETIENNE; RAILWAY TRAINS, PARTS OF; ROCKETS; SHIPS AND BOATS, PARTS OF; STEAMBOATS; WATT, JAMES.

Enola Gay

Probably the most famous airplane of World War II, the *Enola Gay* dropped the first atomic bomb. The mission resulted in the utter destruction of the Japanese city of Hiroshima and marked the start of the nuclear age.

The *Enola Gay* was a U.S. Air Force B-29 Superfortress, the largest bomber built during the war. The plane's range and carrying capacity made it ideal for bombing missions against distant targets. During 1944 and 1945, American B-29 raids launched from airfields in the Pacific islands devastated Japanese cities. The fire-bombing attack on Tokyo in March 1945 killed over 80,000 people. Still the Japanese refused to surrender.

Then in mid-July 1945, American scientists completed the atomic bomb, and soon after President Harry S. Truman approved its use against Japan. The *Enola Gay*—named after the mother of its pilot, Colonel Paul Tibbets, Jr.—was outfitted to carry "Little Boy," a 5-ton atomic bomb. At 9:11 A.M. on August 6, the plane began its bombing run over Hiroshima. When the plane reached an altitude of 31,600 feet (9,630 m), the bomb was released. The bomb exploded about 2,000 feet (610 m) above the city.

As the *Enola Gay* flew on, the crew felt a massive shock wave. The explosion, which burned an area measuring 4.4 square miles (11.4 sq km), killed some 70,000 people. Japan did not surrender to the Allies, however, until a second atomic bomb was dropped on the city of Nagasaki three days later. *See also* AIRCRAFT, MILITARY.

Equator

The equator is a circle around the Earth, with every point along its length an equal distance from the north and south poles. Although the line of the equator is imaginary, it is a vital reference for geographers, mapmakers, and navigators and consequently plays a role in transportation.

In geographic terms, the equator divides the world into the Northern and Southern Hemispheres. In terms of navigation, it is the starting point for the measurement of **latitude,** which is 0 degrees at the equator. The distance around the globe at the equator is 24,902 miles (40,070 km).

latitude distance north or south of the equator

The equatorial zone—the region around the equator—is the hottest part of the planet. Warm air from this zone rises into the atmosphere, becomes cooler, and then sinks down again at the poles. This process creates much of the air circulation that shapes the world's wind and weather patterns. The rising air leaves behind a band of low **atmospheric pressure,** where relatively calm winds—known as the doldrums—form. The doldrums have often slowed the progress of sailing ships crossing the oceans near the equator.

atmospheric pressure pressure exerted by the Earth's atmosphere at any given point on the planet's surface

The Earth really has two equators—the geographic equator, which separates the Northern and Southern Hemispheres, and the magnetic equator. It also has two sets of north and south poles. The magnetic equator is a circle that lies at an equal distance from the two magnetic poles, which are not in the same locations as the geographic poles. Navigators need to be aware of the differences between these two equators and the two sets of poles in order to interpret the readings of magnetic compasses correctly. *See also* AIR CURRENT AND WIND; COMPASS; LATITUDE AND LONGITUDE; NAVIGATION.

Erie Canal

The Erie Canal, an artificial waterway, was built by New York State to connect the Hudson River and the Great Lakes. Completed in 1825, it had a dramatic effect on freight transportation and passenger travel and set off a flurry of canal building in the United States.

Building the Canal. Since colonial times, Americans had searched for good routes between the cities and ports of the East Coast and the interior, regions separated by the ranges of the Appalachian mountain system. In the early 1800s DeWitt Clinton, mayor of New York City, convinced the state legislature to construct a canal between Buffalo, at the eastern end of Lake Erie, and Albany, on the Hudson River. Together the river and the canal would provide a water highway linking the Great Lakes to the Atlantic—and to the world.

The canal faced many obstacles. Some of the proposed route lay through wild forests, and the United States had few engineers and construction firms with the necessary skills and experience. But at the urging

Built between 1817 and 1825, the Erie Canal created a waterway linking the Great Lakes and the Atlantic Ocean. Early barges were towed by horses and mules along the canal.

Life on the Canal

The Erie Canal became a way of life for the people who worked or traveled on it regularly. The waterway had its own culture—its own history, stories, and songs. As the boats moved slowly along the canal, crew members and mule-team drivers passed the time by telling tales and singing songs such as "The E-ri-e" and "The Erie Canal." They sang about the people they met, the towns they passed, the storms they weathered, and the mules that towed the barges. Refrains such as "You'll always know your neighbor,/You'll always know your pal,/If you ever navigated on the Erie Canal" recall this special atmosphere.

aqueduct artificial channel for carrying water

of Clinton—who became governor of New York in 1817—the canal builders overcame all difficulties. Engineers and mechanics working on the project redesigned their tools or invented new equipment to solve problems such as dredging the waterway or removing stubborn tree stumps and roots.

Construction began in 1817 in the town of Rome in central New York and proceeded in both directions. When completed in 1825, the canal was 363 miles (584 km) long, 40 feet (12 m) wide, and 4 feet (1.2 m) deep. Among its notable features were 82 locks, which raised the canal's water level more than 500 feet (152 m) between the Hudson River and Buffalo, and 18 stone **aqueducts,** to carry the canal across obstacles such as the Genesee River.

Effects of the Canal. The Erie Canal was an immediate success. Passenger boats could move along it as fast as 100 miles (161 km) a day. Before the canal was built, farmers in Buffalo paid $100 to ship a ton of produce by land to the Atlantic Coast. After the canal opened, the cost dropped to $10. Long strings of barges, towed by horses or mules that plodded along paths on the canal's banks, carried freight in both directions. Wheat, flour, lumber, pork, whiskey, cheese, and other agricultural products moved east toward markets and ports, while manufactured goods, salt, furniture, and machinery moved west. Syracuse, Utica, and other towns along the route blossomed into flourishing cities.

The planners had predicted the canal would be a great freight highway, but it became an artery for heavy passenger traffic as well. During the mid-1840s, nearly 100,000 people each year made the five-day journey in passenger boats called packets. Many of them were European immigrants headed for the fast-growing Midwest.

The canal had cost the state of New York more than $7 million. By charging tolls for the use of the canal, the state made back its investment within ten years, then turned a handsome profit. Although the success of the Erie Canal inspired other states to build waterways, the spread of railroads after the 1850s ended the growth of canals. During the early 1900s New York repaired and enlarged the Erie Canal as part of the New York State Barge Canal System. *See also* CANALS.

Escalators

see Elevators and Escalators.

Eurail System

The European Rail Network, commonly called Eurail, is an extensive system made up of the national railroads of 17 countries. European trains are fast, clean, and comfortable and known for on-time arrival. Almost every sizable town has a rail station, and ferry services link the rail networks over bodies of water such as the English Channel and the Baltic Sea between Germany and Sweden.

Rail travel is popular in Europe for several reasons. High gasoline prices make long automobile trips expensive. In most cities and towns there are good public transportation services, and visitors do not need their own cars. In addition, the vast network of rail lines—which reaches over 30,000 towns—makes it easy for travelers to find a convenient route to any destination.

Most Eurail trains offer a choice of first- and second-class seating. On long trips, passengers can enjoy meals in a dining car and, on certain trains, can reserve sleeping accommodations for an additional fee. The system includes several high-speed rail lines, such as Germany's Inter City Express, that provide fast transport between major cities and from one country to another.

Since 1959 the Eurail system has offered Eurailpasses, discount passes for unlimited travel on participating railroads for a fixed period. The passes are also valid on certain European shipping lines. Using network trains and ferry connections, passengers can cross the continent—from Ireland to Greece or from Finland to Spain—within the Eurail system. British Rail is not part of the system but offers a BritRail Pass. *See also* CHANNEL TUNNEL; HIGH-SPEED TRAINS; RAILROAD INDUSTRY.

European Space Agency

The European Space Agency (ESA) is a cooperative space program involving 14 nations of Western Europe. It was established in 1975 by merging two agencies: the European Launcher Development Organization (ELDO) and the European Space Research Organization (ESRO). Headquartered in Paris, ESA develops rockets, spacecraft, satellites, instruments, and experiments for space exploration.

In 1980 ESA established a private organization, *Arianespace,* to market the launching of satellites into orbit with ESA's *Ariane* rocket. ESA also oversaw the construction of *Spacelab,* a space laboratory that first went into orbit aboard the U.S. space shuttle *Columbia* in 1983. Two years later ESA launched the space probe *Giotto,* which passed within 370 miles (595 km) of Halley's Comet in 1986 and sent photos and other information about the comet to Earth. ESA has also established a system of weather satellites known as Meteosat.

ESA astronauts work with the Russian and American space programs and have participated in a number of their missions. ESA built a special camera for the Hubble Space Telescope, which was launched into orbit in 1990. The same year the ESA space probe *Ulysses* left the Earth on a mission to orbit the Sun and study its poles. Other ESA satellites study solar winds and the Earth's surface and atmosphere. ESA is also involved in the construction of parts of the new international space station and in training astronauts to spend time on it. *See also* SATELLITES; SPACE EXPLORATION.

Index

Index